NIGER

Rabah Seffal

MARSHALL CAVENDISH
New York • London • Sydney

Reference edition reprinted 2000 by
Marshall Cavendish Corporation
99 White Plains Road
Tarrytown
New York 10591

Originated and designed by
Times Books International, an imprint of
Times Media Private Limited, a member of the
Times Publishing Group

Printed in Singapore

Library of Congress Cataloging-in-Publication Data:

Seffal, Rabah.
    Niger / Rabah Seffal.
        p. cm. — (Cultures of the world)
    Includes bibliographical references and index.
    Summary: A history and geography as well as a description
    of the government, economy, people, lifestyle, religion,
    language, arts, leisure time activities, festivals, and food of
    this landlocked West African country.
    ISBN 0-7614-0995-5 (lib. bdg.)
    1. Niger—Juvenile literature. [1. Niger.] I. Title.
II. Series.

DT547.22 .S44 2001
966.26—dc21   99-055064
                        CIP
                         AC

INTRODUCTION

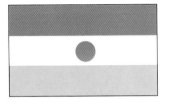

Lying in the southern part of the Sahara, Niger is a landlocked West African country, a link between North Africa and the rest of Africa. Most of Niger's northern part is covered with barren desert and mountains. The southwest, along the banks of the Niger River, is a grassy plain. In the south are steppes that stretch from Chad west along the border with Nigeria. Niger, a predominantly agricultural country, is located in one of the hottest regions of the world, where temperatures sometimes reach 113°F (45°C).

Once a French colony, Niger gained its independence in 1960. The five major ethnic groups constitute about 95% of the population. They include the Hausa, the Songhai and Djerma, the Fulani, the Tuareg, and the Kanouri. Although most Nigeriens practice Islam, there are a small percentage of people who retain traditional animist beliefs or are Christians.

CONTENTS

Stacks of harvested millet awaiting storage.

CONTENTS

Nigerien children pose for a picture.

GEOGRAPHY

THE REPUBLIC OF NIGER is the second largest country in West Africa. The country was named after the Niger River, the third largest river of Africa. Meandering over 2,598 miles (4,184 km) through West Africa, the Niger River flows through the southwestern part of Niger. The name is derived from a word in the Tuareg language—*igher n igheren* ("EEG-er-n-EEG-ar-ain")—which means "river of rivers."

Niger is Africa's 10th largest country. Its total land area is slightly less than twice the size of Texas. Along with Mali and Burkina Faso, it is one of three landlocked countries on the African continent. Niger's neighbors include Algeria on the northwest, Libya on the northeast, Chad on the east, Nigeria on the south, Benin and Burkina Faso on the southwest, and Mali on the west. As the north and northeast are arid and thus uninhabitable, Niger's population is concentrated in the southern part of the country.

Niger has a total land area of 489,062 square miles (1,267,000 square km).

Left: **Nigeriens working on the banks of the Niger River. Many activities are concentrated on this main river.**

Opposite: **Most of the trees that grow in the desert have thick trunks, used to store water.**

Tahoua, in the southern tip of the Sahel, during the rainy season.

TOPOGRAPHY

Niger is located north of Africa's belt of tropical forest. Most of the country is desert. Although primarily a flat plain, the country has several depressions, plateaus, sandy lowlands, fossilized river valleys, and volcanic mountains.

Niger is naturally divided into three distinct regions: the south, the Sahelian belt, and the desert north. The southwest region near the Niger River has an average altitude of 1,067 feet (325 m) above sea level. The arid transitional center, called the Sahel, has a seasonal rainfall and is most suitable for nomadic animal husbandry. It separates the fertile land of the Niger River valley from the harsh desert of the north. The north includes the Aïr Mountains and the plateaus of Djado, Tchigaï, and Mangueni, as well as the Saharan sandy lowlands surrounding the Aïr Mountains.

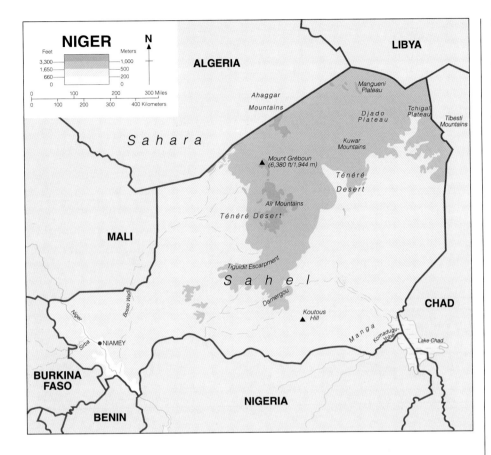

THE SOUTH

This area, which includes the fertile region around the Niger River, consists of a broad plain with an area of 46,320 square miles (120,000 square km), or about 10% of the total land area of Niger. The altitude in this area varies between 985 and 1,149 feet (300 to 350 m) above sea level. As the country's most intensively cultivated area, the population density in the south averages 181 people per square mile (70 per square km). The overall average density for the entire country is only 19.8 people per square mile (7.6 per square km), as the north of Niger is sparsely populated.

To the southeast, Niger's territory includes 988 square miles (2,560 square km) of Lake Chad, Africa's fourth largest lake, which it shares with Nigeria and Chad. Lying along part of the border with Nigeria is the Komadugu-Yobe River, which flows into Lake Chad.

THE SAHEL

Separating the desert-like north from the fertile south is the Sahel, an arid region with very little rainfall. Sahel means "shore" in Arabic—the area is the shore of the "sea of sand" of the Sahara. This region is usually divided into the north Sahel belt, which includes the city of Agadez, and the south Sahel belt. Agricultural activities in the Agadez region are only possible in oases. The south Sahel belt has a rainfall pattern that allows crops to be grown for four months of the year. The area also supports grazing for the cattle of the nomadic herders. Although the Sahel belts can be relatively self-sufficient in good years, during severe droughts, its inhabitants suffer greatly.

A camel train crossing the desert.

THE NORTH

North of the Sahel and the city of Agadez lies the spectacular Aïr Mountains, a southern extension of the Algerian Ahaggar Mountains. The Aïr contain many rock paintings made by Stone Age people. With an area of approximately 30,880 square miles (80,000 square km) and an average elevation of up to 2,625 feet (800 m), the Aïr is intersected by several ravines where date palms, dum-dum palms, and desert bushes flourish. In the Aïr, Mount Gréboun is Niger's highest peak. It towers at 6,380 feet (1,944 m).

East of the Aïr Mountains is the Ténéré, which means "desert" in Tamasheqt, the language of the Tuareg people. The total area of the Ténéré is 154,400 square miles (400,000 square km). It offers a magnificent landscape of sand dunes that seem to stretch to the horizon. Tuareg caravans from Agadez still travel to the oases that punctuate the Ténéré dunes, trading for salt.

To the west of the Aïr, the Talak Desert consists of shifting sand dunes interrupted by ancient river valleys, like those found in the Aïr Mountains. About 6,000 years ago, water used to flow in these valleys, allowing the desert north of Niger to support a larger population. Now the grasslands of this region attract nomadic cattle herders, but only during the short rainy seasons.

Northeast of the Ténéré lie the high plateaus of Djado and Tchigaï, and the Mangueni Mountains, an extension of the Tibesti Mountains of Chad to the east and the Ahaggar Mountains of Algeria to the north. These highlands form a bridge linking the two mountain systems.

The majestic Aïr Mountains have volcanic origins.

11

DESTRUCTIVE DROUGHTS

With a highly variable climate, the Sahel poses a threat to the long-term survival of its inhabitants. During the 19th century, the human and animal populations grew rapidly due to a higher-than-normal rainfall. Then the Sahel suffered a severe drought between 1911 and 1914, which killed more than 350,000 people in central Niger alone.

Even after the country gained independence in 1960, the situation did not improve. From 1968 to 1974 another drought wiped out livestock and crippled the social and economic system of the area, especially that of the nomadic herders. The drought effects included food shortages in following years. Again in 1984 a drought brought extensive suffering to the country.

CLIMATE AND RAINFALL

Niger is one of the hottest countries in the world. Climatically it has three regions: the desert north, the Sahel, and the south. The desert north, including the Ténéré, receives little rainfall, offering neither agricultural nor cattle herding possibilities except in oases and the old river valleys of the Talak. South of the desert, the north Sahel has a maximum of 14 inches (35 cm) of annual rainfall. In Agadez annual rainfall does not exceed 7 inches (18 cm). The south Sahel receives 12 to 32 inches (30 to 80 cm) of rainfall per year. In the south, a rainy season from June to October is preceded by violent tornadoes. In the extreme south, around Gaya, rainfall averages 32 inches (80 cm) per year.

During the dry season, from January to October, temperatures are very high. From November the temperature starts to drop, falling as low as 46°F (8°C) in January. In November a desert wind, the harmattan, lowers average temperatures to 70°F (21°C). Reddish sandstorms sweep across the country during this period. From February to July the dry and hot season sets in, with temperatures reaching a scorching 122°F (50°C) in the northeast.

FLORA AND FAUNA

Because of Niger's climate, flora and fauna vary dramatically from the dry north to the wetter and more fertile south. Like its Sahelian neighbors, Niger is suffering from ecological degradement. Irregular rainfall and periodic droughts threaten animal populations and plant life.

The desert north, which covers 60% of Niger's land surface, has little vegetation. However, in Bilma, abundant springs allow some tree species, such as Eucalypti, to flourish. On the northern rim of the Aïr Mountains, several types of Mediterranean plants, such as Laperrine olive and cypresses, have survived. In the Sahel, thorns, Mimoseae, Graminaceae, and scattered pastures of grass have a short life and provide good grazing material for both nomadic and settled herds. A useful plant is the areleshem, sought after by the camels. The areleshem has oval-shaped leaves and white, bud-like flowers. The Tuareg use the flowers as a cure for stomachache. To the south, a denser vegetation is found that includes baobab trees. Silk cotton, mahogany, and shea trees can be found.

A dry forest near Gaya, which is located just north of Niger's border with Benin.

13

A crane in the "W" National Park. The nature reserve is so named because the Niger River flows through it in the shape of a "W." The park is shared by Niger, Burkina Faso, and Benin.

In the north, the lack of water and vegetation coupled with extremely high temperatures, limits the types of wildlife. The largest animal is the one-humped camel. Its broad, leathery foot pads are well adapted to the desert. Besides the domesticated camel, wild animals, such as antelopes and gazelles, are found in the Ténéré and the Aïr regions. These animals are the favorite prey of leopards, striped hyenas, and jackals.

The smaller desert animals in Niger include desert foxes or fennecs, which prey on jerboas or desert mice. The sensitive fennec has large, pointed ears and can hear a desert beetle kick over sand grains several yards away. Moufflons can be found in the inaccessible terrain of the Aïr Mountains and Djado Plateau. South of the Sahara, ostriches, the world's tallest birds, live in hot, sandy areas. The males are polygamous and travel in multifamily groups. Eggs are laid in sandy depressions and incubated by females during the day; by males at night. Desert animals eat a large number of insects, including the migratory locusts, as well as scorpions and vipers.

Although droughts and poaching have taken their toll on Niger's wildlife, some large mammals, such as elephants, giraffes, and hippopotami, and reptiles and amphibians still exist. The nature reserve and wildlife refuge of the "W" National Park is home to monkeys, baboons, hyenas, jackals, lions, elephants, buffalos, antelopes, and gazelles. Birdlife, including the brown crow, is also abundant there. The nomads herd cattle, sheep, goats, donkeys, and camels. Camels are also used as a means of transportation by caravans, especially by the salt traders.

MAJOR CITIES

NIAMEY "*Way niammanē*" or "Settle and acquire" was an order given by a Djerma leader named Kallé to his subjects when they saw a vast uninhabited region next to the river. The city later was named Niamma and then Niamey. In 1926 a French general saw the strategic potential of Niamey as the capital. Access to the river and the moderate climate in this city made the French transfer their administrative capital from Zinder to Niamey. Until then, Niamey was not an economically or politically important city.

Niamey began as a conglomeration of several villages that grew and joined to become one city. In 1905 the population was only 1,800. It grew to 7,000 in 1945. Today, with a population of 500,000, Niamey is a sprawling modern center with shantytowns on the outskirts. No skycrapers are found, but in the residential areas next to the ministerial offices, there are some beautiful villas. Traditional-style African houses also neatly line the streets.

Niger's capital, Niamey, is located along the fertile strip of land bordering the 300-mile (483-km) Niger River.

The city of Zinder.

ZINDER With a population of 82,000 people, Zinder is a typical Hausa town with a narrow maze of alleys. Connected to Niamey by a monotonous 450-mile (725-km) "unity road," it competes with other major cities for the title of the second most important city in Niger. Several roads connect Zinder with the city of Kano in Nigeria. A few small industries are located in Zinder. They concentrate on the processing of farm products and the manufacturing of small industrial products.

The neighborhood of Zengou, in Zinder, is a former caravan encampment. Until the 1890s, Zinder was Niger's only major urban settlement, with a population of about 10,000. Built around a citadel, it was a major point of exchange and storage for the TransSaharan trade route. Precolonial Zinder was home to the Hausa kingdom of Damagram, which was a strong economic power. In 1898 the French captain, Cazamajou, on a mission to neutralize Zinder, was killed. Zinder put up a heavy resistance to French invasion, ultimately falling in 1899. It remained the administrative capital of the French Military Territory of Niger until 1926, and an old French foreign legion fort stills stands in the city today.

AGADEZ Located in the Aïr Mountains, about 400 miles (644km) northeast of Niamey, Agadez was the ancient Tuareg capital. The city still preseves its trading caravans and the myths surrounding that life. It is a town built at the edge of the desert that serves as the link between the free but treacherous desert life and the limited but safe urban life. The Hausa of Gobir, who fled Tuareg raiders in the sixth century, live in Agadez. The TransSaharan gold trade route to North Africa passed through Agadez and brought prosperity and strength to local rulers. The Empire of Mali occupied Agadez for 50 years from 1325. The city fell to the powerful Songhai Empire in the 16th century. Sultans El-Mobarek and Agaba ruled Agadez from 1654 until 1721. In 1906 the French occupied the city.

Today Agadez is a meeting point for all Tuareg groups and a living center for the preservation of their ancient history. With a population of 20,000, Agadez is sometimes referred to as the sister city of Timbuktu in Mali. The color of its distinctive sand-brick architecture matches that of the desert dunes. Its people are mainly Tuareg, but the population also includes Fulani nomads and Hausa merchants.

The population of Agadez increased significantly after the discovery of uranium, which boosted the economy of the north.

HISTORY

NIGER HAS HAD A LONG, TUMULTUOUS HISTORY. From ethnic struggles to independence, the country has faced many years of foreign dominance and civil strife.

EARLY INHABITANTS

Stone tools, evidence of a Paleolithic culture, indicate the presence of humans more than 60,000 years ago in the Aïr, Ténéré, Djado, and Kuwar regions. The stone tools, including axes, discs, and stone knives, were produced by a Neolithic Saharan culture that domesticated bulls and herded cattle, an activity still practiced today by the different nomadic groups of Niger. Artists of the Neolithic Saharan culture probably drew the numerous rock paintings, frequently found north of Agadez.

Left: **Many of the rock paintings found in the Aïr Mountains depicted cattle, hunters using chariots, and horsemen.**

Opposite: **The ancient mosque of Agadez, built in the 16th century.**

19

Many of the settlements of the early kingdoms were located along the Niger River.

THE SAVANNA KINGDOMS

THE ZAGHAWA KINGDOM was located around the Chad Basin from A.D. 700 to 1100 and included the North Kanem region, northeast of Lake Chad. The term Zaghawa does not refer to a specific culture or period but to the pre-Islamic black inhabitants of the kingdom. The Zaghawa were the first to acquire the skills of casting iron, develop the art of making crafts, and provide services to the nomadic and sedentary groups around Kanem. They relied on agriculture, fishing, and making crafts for a living, and in a later period, international trade, which included slaves, with the Muslim states of North Africa and the Middle East. An economic transformation led to the rise of the Kanem Empire after the 12th century.

THE HABASHA KINGDOM consisted predominantly of Chadic speakers, who lived on the river valleys around the same time as the Zaghawa. Like them, the Habasha traded and sold their agricultural produce as well as other crafts and were not just subsistence farmers. Most were cattle herders and salt traders. The Habasha were not ambitious. As the Zaghawa kingdom expanded to the west, the Habasha kingdom contracted into the kingdoms of Gobir and Katsina. As the Mbau tribe on its southern border developed, the Habasha joined them to form what was later known as the Mbau kingdom. The term "Mbau" refers to the original inhabitants of the savanna region between Niger and Nigeria. Although traces of their history are found today in the numerous village names, their language is almost extinct. The Mbau people were much feared for their raids.

Toward the seventh century A.D., the first Songhai and Kanem states appeared in the western and the eastern parts of Niger respectively. With its capital in Gao, Mali, the Songhai Empire expanded its territory along the Niger River, while the Kanem Empire concentrated its rule around Lake Chad and extended its conquest north to the Fezzan in Libya. In between the two empires, smaller states, such as the Hausa state, were formed. Around A.D. 1000, an increase in economic relations with North Africa via the Aïr region led to migrations of Tuareg from Libya and Algeria toward the Aïr and adjacent regions. At this time, both the Songhai and Kanem empires adopted Islam as their religion. Meanwhile, the Hausa, who previously lived in the north, gradually moved south.

Zinder was the capital of the Damagaran state. In the mid-19th century, its ruler, Ténimoum, erected a 3-mile (5-km) wall around the city. According to legend, this majestic wall would never collapse because a number of Korans, the Muslim holy book, and virgin girls were "built" into the walls. Over the years, the wall has broken down, and all that remains are ruins.

THE 16TH TO 19TH CENTURIES

In the 16th century, Niger was greatly influenced by the Songhai and Bornu empires. The Bornu Empire reached its apex under the rule of Idris Alauna (1571–1603). The acme of Songhai rule occurred during the reign of Askia Mohammed (1493–1528), who in 1498, went on a pilgrimage to the Muslim holy city of Mecca. The journey helped consolidate his rule.

The Songhai Empire was destroyed by Moroccans who came to search for the gold of Sudanic Africa, and who wanted to control the trade routes. The battle of Tondibi in 1591 was a heavy loss for the Songhai as it was their first encounter with the use of gunpowder and muskets. Nine years later, the Moroccans were forced out of Dendi. Despite this, the Songhai Askia dynasty soon collapsed and fragmented into smaller and weaker states. The Songhai Empire never regained its previous grandeur.

In the 19th century, the Hausa state of Damagaran in the east became a great military and economic power. Zinder was their capital, and manufacturing and new agricultural products were introduced.

THE SUPERPOWERS OF THE 16TH CENTURY

THE SONGHAI EMPIRE was one of the greatest empires of West Africa. Its dominance reached a peak when Sonni Ali took power and lasted more than 100 years. The dominant individuals of the Songhai were the Sorko fishermen. Known as the "masters of waters," the Sorko navigated the waters of Niger River from Dendi, reaching places north of Tillabéry. A cohesive and important political organization was born among them, resulting in the first Songhai dynasty known as the Dya. By the eighth century A.D., increased economic relations with the Kharedjite Tahert state in western Algeria strengthened the Songhai kingdom. The city of Gao became the commercial center and the residence of the Songhai rulers. Kukiya, southeast of Gao, remained the ancestral capital where festivals and royal celebrations took place.

Around the mid-12th century, the Empire of Mali attempted to extend its rule over all Sahara the trade route terminals. However as a remote province, Songhai attempted to gain its independence amid periods of weakness in Mali. Under the leader of Ali Kolon, the new dynasty of the Sonni was founded. But it was not until the beginning of the 15th century that the Songhai Empire started to build its military power and begin expansion under the rule of Sonni Ali the Great (1464–1492). Spreading westward, it conquered Timbuktu in 1469 and Jene in 1473. As the Empire of Mali retreated south of the Niger Delta, having lost its Sahelian territory, the Songhai Empire, during the rule of Askia Muhammad (1493–1528), acquired additional former provinces of Mali. It also conquered the Berber city of Agadez and the Hausa states on the southern border of today's Niger. The end of the 15th century saw the destruction of the Songhai Empire when the North African empire of Morocco conquered its territory.

THE EMPIRE OF BORNU benefited greatly from the collapse of the Kanem Empire. The latter empire fell due to the lack of resources, royal rivalry, and internal conflicts, which erupted in the mid-13th century. Even before the collapse of Kanem, parts of Bornu had become independent, especially after the Bornu economy started to benefit from the direct TransSaharan trade route to North Africa. In the 14th century, when the Suffewa rulers started to encounter opposition from the Bulala, a rival dynasty, the Suffewa rulers and their followers left Kanem and headed toward Bornu, where they had long before placed lords.

Despite fleeing from Kanem, the Suffewa's conflict with the Bulala continued for many years. The Suffewa later solved their internal problems and regained strength and security from 1465–1497 under the rule of Ali Dunama, also called Gaji "the Younger." He was able to resolve the struggle for the throne between the different branches of the Suffewa. In addition, Ali Gagi ended the threat of the Bulala once and for all and laid the foundation of a new and powerful Suffewa Mais dynasty, with its capital at Gzargamo. The Suffewa in Bornu saw in Islam a powerful means of strengthening their authority over the Bornu lands. As the different groups accepted Islam, stability was restored.

A Tuareg salt caravan bivouac in the desert. They had encountered a sandstorm.

THE TUAREG DOMINATION

As a result of an improved economy spurred by the trade routes through the Sahara, the influence of the Tuaregs grew. They established their first sultanate in the Aïr Mountains as early as the beginning of 15th century. Agadez, in the southern part of the Aïr Mountains, became their economic and cultural center, attracting merchants from North Africa. As the center grew in economic importance, the role of the Tuaregs became more of an arbiter than a guardian of the caravan traffic. Their control stretched to Gao and Timbuktu in the west and to Tadmakka in Mali.

In the Aïr Mountains, from 1654 to 1687, the Tuaregs were ruled by Mohammed Al-Mubarek, who extended his authority to the Damergou region. He also established a branch of the Agadez dynasty that later became the empire of Sarkin Adar in the late 17th century. As Tuareg dominance grew, there were frequent internal conflicts, which divided them into several factions. But as they gained control of more regions, they started to appreciate the advantages of being a large-scale organization.

An old French hotel in Niger.

THE FRENCH CONQUEST

In the 19th century, as a prelude to their conquest, Europeans started to explore Niger. In 1890 an agreement between France and Great Britain at a meeting with King Leopold II established the border between what was to become Niger and Nigeria. The agreement also set out spheres of influence. France then started its conquest of the country but met with strong resistance. In Zinder, Sultan Ahmadu Kuren Daga ordered the execution of French captain Cazemajou in 1898.

Subsequent armed exploration by French captains Paul Voulet and Charles Chanoine resulted in bloody massacres and the destruction of cities and villages, before the country was conquered. Throughout the years of French domination, the local population continued to fight the French. The Zarama uprising (1905–1906) and the Tuareg resistance (1916–1917) resulted in much bloodshed. British troops were brought in to assist the French, and the Tuareg suffered a major defeat. In 1922, when peace was finally restored, Niger became a French colony.

During the colonial period, peanuts were the only cash crop.

ROAD TO INDEPENDENCE

Niger was administered from Paris through the governor-general in Dakar, Senegal. The lack of natural resources in Niger limited French investment, compared to other French West African colonies. As France decentralized its political power after World War II, Nigeriens were theoretically granted full citizenship in 1946, but their participation in local politics was limited.

A nationalist movement soon gained momentum. In a split in the early 1950s, two groups formed—a radical group with a strong trade union, led by Djibo Bakary, and a more conservative movement, the Nigerien Progressive Party, that supported Hamani Diori. Diori won the Territorial Assembly elections in 1958. He formed a government and banned Bakary's Sawaba party. On September 28, 1958, the Nigerien population approved the constitution of General De Gaulle's Fifth French Republic. On December 19, 1958, Niger's Territorial Assembly voted for Niger to become an autonomous state within the French community, to be called the Republic of Niger. On August 3, 1960, Niger declared its independence.

AFTER INDEPENDENCE

When Niger gained its independence, Hamani Diori became the country's first president. The first Nigerien constitution was approved on November 8, 1960. As the sole party, the Niger Progressive Party (PPN) became firmly established throughout the country, including the rural areas. The government's program of political democratization was resisted by students and civil service groups. The drought of 1973 dealt a severe blow to the economy, and internal problems remained unsolved. On April 15, 1974, Lieutenant-Colonel Seyni Kountché staged a military coup. He succeeded in suspending the constitution, dissolving the PPN, and arresting its leaders. Diori was replaced by Kountché.

Kountché formed a provisional government, which was led by the Supreme Military Council. He maintained cordial relations with France, Niger's former colonizer, despite the fact that he expelled French troops. The late 1980s saw a significant increase in revenue from uranium, which allowed Niger to recover financially from the drought. Following Kountché's death in 1987, Colonel Ali Seybou was appointed president.

In November 1991, the transitional government of Amadou Acheffou replaced President Seybou, and the Tuaregs revolted in the north amid rumors that the government had embezzled international funds meant for the resettlement of the Tuareg population who had fled during the severe droughts. Both parties consequently signed several peace treaties, but the truces were short-lived. In January 1996 Colonel Ibrahim Baré Maïnassara overthrew the elected government of Mahamane Ousmane, putting an end to democracy. He was elected president in July with 52% of the votes. Maïnassara was assassinated on April 9, 1999 at the Niamey airport. A national Reconciliation Council was formed, and Commandant Daouda Malam Wanké became the president of Niger on April 11, 1999.

Djibo Bakary and Hamani Diori, both Songhai-Djermas, were cousins.

GOVERNMENT

AFTER NIGER GAINED ITS INDEPENDENCE IN 1960, the country was run by the Niger Progressive Party, or Parti Progressiste Nigérien (PPN), under the leadership of Hamani Diori. He consolidated party power by banning the opposition party, the Sawaba. The 1970 drought, coupled with protests initiated by unions and students, weakened the government, which was subsequently overthrown by a military coup in 1974. In 1989 presidential and legislative elections were held for the newly formed MNSD (National Movement for the Development of Society) to anchor its power.

However, Tuareg revolts and attacks, student demonstrations, and union and civil society unrest forced the government to hold a free, multiparty election in 1993. In 1996 the Nigerien Armed Forces staged a coup, claiming they were saving the country from disintegration, the result of a paralyzed political system caused by the civilian government.

Left: **The former French prime minister, M. Debre, with four African leaders in Paris. On the far left is Hamani Diori, the first president of Niger.**

Opposite: **The Nigerien National Assembly Building.**

LOCAL GOVERNMENT

The country is divided into seven territorial units called *départments* ("day-PART-mahn") and one capital district, which is Niamey. The *départments* are subdivided into 38 districts, called *arrondissements* ("ah-RAWN-dees-mahn"), and are run by a chief administrator, called a *préfet* ("PRAY-fay"). The *préfet* is appointed by the central government in Niamey and acts as the *départments'* local agent.

The seven départments include Agadez, Diffa, Dosso, Maradi, Tahoua, Tillaberi, and Zinder.

THE PRESIDENT

The 1993 constitution, approved in a referendum, provides for the election of a president with executive powers for a five-year term. He can stay in office for a maximum of two terms. Elected by popular vote, the president is both the chief of state and head of the government. He appoints a prime minister and a 27-member cabinet of ministers on the recommendation of the prime minister.

The right of the Nigeriens to elect their government was granted in the 1993 constitution. Nevertheless, the January 1996 military coup, subsequent presidential elections, and a constitutional referendum election prevented Nigeriens from fully exercising that right. One of the most important constitutional changes in 1993 was an increase in the power of the president.

The president rules by decree when the National Assembly is not in session. The executive branch appoints members of the judiciary, officials of the security forces, and heads of state-owned companies. The legislative branch is the unicameral National Assembly, which has 83 members elected for five-year terms. The president can initiate legislation either by proposing an act to the National Assembly or by submitting it to a popular referendum.

THE CONSTITUTION

On November 8, 1960, the constitution of an independent Niger was promulgated, establishing a presidential regime. Following the coup in 1974, this constitution was suspended, and the National Assembly dissolved. All executive and legislative power was held by the Supreme Military Council until 1989. In 1993 a new constitution was adopted. When the government was overthrown by Colonel Ibrahim Maïnassara in 1996, the constitution was revised by national referendum on May 12, 1996.

The Nigerien constitution separates church and state, and guarantees the political, cultural, and religious freedom of its citizens, with the right to form associations. Nigeriens have the freedom to travel in and out of the country. Under the new constitution, suspects cannot be arrested without due process of the law.

The president's palace.

THE MILITARY

Niger's armed forces consists of five branches: the army, air force, national police, National Gendarmerie, and the Republican Guard. As a landlocked country, Niger does not have a navy. The total active duty personnel includes 5,200 army soldiers and 100 air force personnel who operate 12 airplanes. There are 2,500 Republican Guards, 1,500 national policemen, and 1,400 soldiers in the National Gendarmerie.

Most of Niger's military equipment comes from France, with whom it has bilateral defense agreements. A selective number of Nigeriens age 18 and above have to serve the military for two years. Recent implementation of peace accords between the government and leaders of the Tuareg include the integration of the Tuareg fighters into the military forces.

THE FIRST MULTIPARTY ELECTIONS

As the first multiparty legislative elections since independence, the 1993 elections saw the participation of nine political parties. The National Movement for the Development of Society (MNSD), once the sole political Nigerien party, lost the election to a broad alliance of parties. The political party was formed during

Kountché's rule. Mahamane Ousmane, who belonged to the Social and Democratic Convention (CDS), became the first freely elected president of Niger.

The Ousmane presidency was marked by student and civil strikes and the continuing Tuareg revolt in the north. When he failed to accommodate the numerous political groups in the National Assembly, President Ousmane called for new parliamentary elections in 1995. His party, the MNSD, won by a slight majority, gaining 29 seats, while the CDS won 24 seats. A coalition government was formed. However, a tug-of-war developed between President Ousmane and Prime Minister Hama Amadou, paralyzing the government. Army chief Ibrahim Bare Maïnassara stepped in and overthrew Ousmane, ending Niger's first democratic government. Presidential elections were held in July 1996, which were won by Maïnassara.

When Maïnassara was later assassinated, a National Reconciliation Council was formed, and a squadron commander, Daouda Malam Wanké, was named its president and head of the Nigerien state. He promised a referendum vote on the constitution and elections in late 1999.

Opposite: **A Tuareg rebel, armed with a dagger.**

COMMANDANT WANKÉ

Commandant Daouda Malam Wanké was born in 1954 in Yelou, which is located in the Gaya region, about 106 miles (170 km) south of Niamey. Wanké is a Hausa. From 1974 to 1977, he studied at an Algerian school of engineering. After graduating, he went to the military academy of Antsérabé in Madagascar from 1980 to 1983. He later attended an artillery school in France. He was General Maïnassara's chief of presidential guard and was present when the former president was killed at the airport by a group of 12 officers.

Hamani Diori, leader of the PPN.

POLITICAL PARTIES

NIGERIEN PROGRESSIVE PARTY (PPN)   Formed during the 1946 administrative reforms, the PPN was established in the aftermath of dwindled interest in the African Democratic Rally (RDA), which was supported by labor unions. Under the leadership of Hamani Diori, and with the help of the French administration, it was established as the sole political party when the country gained its independence. In the October 1970 presidential and legislative elections, Diori won 99.98% of the votes, while the PPN won a 97.09% majority. His government was dissolved in 1974 when it was overthrown by the military. Diori was imprisoned until 1980.

NIGER DEMOCRATIC UNION (POPULARLY KNOWN AS THE SAWABA) Djibo Bakara established the Sawaba in 1946. As a radical and neo-Marxist party, the Sawaba favored immediate independence from France. In the 1958 elections, the Sawaba was badly defeated by Diori's PPN. After independence, the ruling PPN banned the Sawaba, and Bakara was exiled. In retaliation Bakara organized two attempts, in 1964 and 1965, to assassinate Diori from exile.

NATIONAL MOVEMENT FOR THE DEVELOPMENT OF SOCIETY (MNSD)   Formed in 1988 by General Seybou, who had succeeded Kountché, the MNSD was the sole political party in Niger until 1991. Faced with overwhelming calls for multiparty democracy, and a general strike lasting two days, the ruling party allowed Niger to have its first multiparty parliamentary and presidential elections. An interim government, headed

GENERAL IBRAHIM BARE MAÏNASSARA

Born in May 1949 in Maradi, the son of a schoolteacher, Maïnassara joined the military when he was 21 years old. After attending the Antsérabé Academy in Madagascar, he rose through the ranks. He took part in the 1974 coup when Kountché overthrew Niger's first president Diori Hamani and became an aide to Kountché at the age of 25. He attended the military school of infantry in Montpellier, France, for a year and was named chief of the presidential guard in 1976. Two years later he took over the supervision of the special parachutists unit in Niamey.

In 1986 Maïnassara became military attaché of the Nigerien embassy in Paris before becoming minister of public health in 1987. He was the Nigerien ambassador in Paris between 1988 and 1990 and then in Algeria from 1990 to 1992.

In 1992 he returned to Niger to become the military advisor to the transition prime minister, Amadou Cheiffou. After the 1993 elections, President Mahamane Ousmane made him chief of staff. After attending the French Interarm Defense College, he was appointed the Nigerien army chief of staff in 1995. He seized power in 1996, putting an end to the democratically elected but politically unstable presidency of Ousmane.

But his rule was short-lived. Demonstrations by civil servants and teachers overshadowed his presidency. During his term, he signed a deal with the International Monetary Fund and introduced economic reforms. The opposition mounted protests, calling for his resignation.

As a Muslim from the Hausa ethnic group, he attempted to allay the fundamentalists by banning Western dress worn by women and clamping down on the sale of contraceptives.

by Amadou Cheiffou, was formed to help the government prepare for the multiparty elections. However, the MNSD failed to gain followers among the Nigerien population. As a result of student and union protests and the Tuareg revolt, the MNSD was forced to accept the establishment of at least 15 other parties. It lost the parliamentary and presidential elections in 1993 when a coalition of nine major opposition parties joined ranks and won control of the parliament and the presidency. In 1995 the MNSD won a majority in parliament when President Ousmane called for early parliamentary elections.

ECONOMY

UNTIL THE 1970s NIGER was considered to be the least resource-endowed country in Africa and one of the 10 poorest countries in the world. This arid and landlocked land can barely sustain the rural population and its agricultural economy. The agricultural activities depend largely on distinct climatic changes in each zone. In some areas droughts create serious food shortages for the population and their livestock, and imports have to be brought in to make up for the shortfall.

The discovery of a massive amount of uranium at Arlit has made Niger the world's second largest uranium exporter, second only to Canada. This significantly boosted Niger's revenues. In the early 1980s, however, a worldwide oversupply of uranium and falling prices forced Niger to tighten its budget. In 1990 Niger's external debt rose past the $1.8 billion mark, and in 1994 France devaluated the CFA currency by half.

Left: **A market in Niamey.**

Opposite: **A trader counts his earnings for the day. The sudden devaluation of the CFA franc in January 1994 boosted Niger's trade relations with Nigeria, and income from exporting livestock, peas, and onions, as well the cotton industry, increased.**

AGRICULTURE

More than 90% of the Nigerien population is engaged in agriculture and in raising livestock. Crops are grown mainly in the south where rainfall is more abundant, and the soils are richer. The dry north and Sahel areas, which receive only seasonal rainfall, are used for nomadic stock raising. Successive droughts in 1971 and 1984 considerably reduced the size of the cattle herds.

Groundnuts, or peanuts, the most important cash crop in Niger, are planted in the sandy soils of Maradi and Zinder. Niger is the third largest peanut grower in Africa. To diversify the economy and reduce Niger's dependence on peanuts, cotton was introduced as a crop in 1956. It is cultivated in the Tahoua region, but high production has failed to materialize because of the lack of incentives to attract farmers.

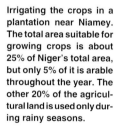

Irrigating the crops in a plantation near Niamey. The total area suitable for growing crops is about 25% of Niger's total area, but only 5% of it is arable throughout the year. The other 20% of the agricultural land is used only during rainy seasons.

Niger's main food crops are sorghum and millet, which are grown on about 90% of the cultivated land. Millet is usually grown by itself in light soil, but sometimes it is planted among rows of peanuts or beans. Sorghum requires a richer soil than millet. A small portion of the millet and sorghum production is exported. Since 1980, there has been an increased interest in vegetables and cereals as cash crops. Another agricultural food crop produced in Niger is onions.

Niger imports cereals, including wheat, rice, corn, millet, and sorghum. The harvest varies as much as 10% from year to year, depending on the amount of rainfall—production fell by 40% during the drought years of 1984–85 and rose by about 5% in the good years of 1988–89. Most of the rice produced is consumed locally. As demand for cassava and beans increases, cultivation of these crops has grown. Nigeriens also grow onions, tomatoes, wheat, and sugarcane. Most of the sugarcane plantations are located near Tillabéry. Wheat is grown in Agadez, near Lake Chad, and in the Aïr and Kuwar mountains. Tomatoes grow well in Tahoua, Zinder, and Agadez.

A busy livestock market. The size of the herds has improved significantly since the drought years, and demand has increased.

HUSBANDRY AND FISHING

Husbandry is Niger's most important activity. Land that is unsuitable for agriculture serves for grazing animals. Herds traditionally move north during the rainy season. The animals are the herders' capital and only resource. Used for transportation, the animals also provide milk, meat, and leather. The leather is used for the awnings of tents, clothes, shoes, and ropes. In a good year, communities can perform social and religious activities, such as making donations, engaging in barter trade, and making sacrifices. In 1997 there were 6.2 million goats, 4.1 million sheep, and 2.1 million cattle in Niger.

The principal herd animal is the zebu, a member of the ox family characterized by lyre-like horns and a relatively large, fleshy hump over its shoulders. The zebu has pendulous ears and a distinct resistance to heat and insect attacks. Other herd animals include goats, sheep, and camels. Fishing activities are limited to areas along the banks of the Niger River and near Lake Chad.

MINING AND INDUSTRY

In 1960 Niger started a program to develop its natural resources. As a result uranium was discovered at Arlit in the Agadez region in 1967. This led to a huge increase in the country's revenues, and money was channeled to the development of infrastructure, industry, communications, and training. Huge coal reserves were also discovered northeast of Agadez. Today, 3,000 tons of uranium are exported annually, making Niger the world's second largest uranium exporter, although royalties do not exceed 10% of the country's revenues. Its principal buyer is France. Besides mining in the north, industrial production includes a manufacturing industry in the south, where factories process agricultural products, such as peanuts, millet, sorghum, cotton, and cattle products. Smaller industrial units focus on making cement and mortar bricks for local consumption.

Bottling drinks in a factory. These industrial companies are usually of a modest size, not large-scale enterprises.

TRANSPORTATION

Possessing no railroads and ports, Niger relies on roads for transportation. Niger's road grid includes east-to-west and north-to-south roads that provide access to neighboring countries. Three main roads connect Niger to Benin, Nigeria, and Burkina Faso. The total length of highways is 6,272 miles (10,100 km), of which only 496 miles (798 km) are paved.

Air Afrique, an airline company jointly owned by West African countries and a few international companies, provides air travel in and out of Niger. The national airline, Air Niger, offers domestic air services between Diffa, Agadez, Tahoua, Zinder, Arlit, and Maradi. The international airport is at Niamey. To transport goods overseas, Niger uses the Cotonou port in Benin and the Lagos port in Nigeria.

Between December and March, the Niger River is navigable for 186 miles (300 km) from Niamey to Gaya, which lies on the border with Benin. Canoes are used to ferry people across rivers. In the rural areas where road networks are less developed, donkeys and camels are used. It is not unusual to see camels crossing the bridges in the capital city of Niamey.

AZALAY, THE 2,500-YEAR-OLD SALT CARAVAN

Originating in the fifth century B.C., the *azalay* ("ah-ZAH-lay") is an ancient system of transportation that refers to a caravan of camels that travels a large distance. Today these legendary caravans still ply the Ténéré Desert and link Agadez to the oases of Bilma and Fachi, which provide salt, dates, and natron. The much sought after natron, a low-grade carbonate of soda found in the oases of Kawar, is consumed by both humans and animals.

Crossing the Ténéré takes about three weeks. The caravans can consist of 10,000 to 20,000 camels and can stretch for 16 miles (25 km). Because they travel over vast distances, these caravans are often subject to attacks by bandits. The caravans are mostly manned by the Tuareg, but other ethnic groups, such as the Hausa and Toubou, are also attracted to this way of life.

These children are fascinated by the new solar-powered television in their village.

POTENTIAL RESOURCES

The Nigerien government is actively promoting its oil potential. Recent geological research has discovered oil fields in the eastern part of the country, near the border with Chad. A number of foreign companies are also exploring for gold. In addition, iron has been found near the south of Niamey, but its high phosphor content and difficulties in transportation make its exploitation uneconomical. Other prospecting has discovered copper, lignite, zinc, chromium, molybdenum, tungsten, lithium, titanium, and phosphates.

The government has built a hydroelectric power station and a coal-burning power station, and its Office of Solar Energy is producing solar batteries, which are used to power the country's telecommunications network.

These children are fascinated by the new solar-powered television in their village.

NIGERIENS

LANGUAGES DISTINGUISH THE PEOPLE OF NIGER, who can be categorized into five language groups: the Hausa, the Djerma-Songhai, the Fulani, the Tuareg, and the Kanouri. The Hausa constitute about 56% of the population, while the Djerma-Songhai form 22%. The Fulani are 8.5% of the population, the Tuareg 8%, and the Kanouri 4.3%. Smaller groups include the Toubou, Arabs, and Gourmantché, which together constitute about 1.2%. There are about 1,200 French expatriates in Niger.

In addition to a common historical heritage, the Muslim religion is the country's other unifying factor. Sunni Muslims predominate in Niger. Another unifying factor is the Hausa language, which is understood by the majority of the Nigerien population. Most of the country's ethnic groups live separately, while maintaining close relationships with their relatives in neighboring countries like Chad and Nigeria.

The total population of Niger is 9,962,242 in 1999.

Left: **Children under the age of 15 form nearly half of the Nigerien population.**

Opposite: **Young Tuareg girls relaxing in their clay house.**

Hausa men with their sons.

THE HAUSA

The Hausa constitute about 56% of the Nigerien population. The Hausa are also present in northern Nigeria where they dominate Nigerian economic and political life. There are about 25 million Hausa people in West Africa. Some of their ancestors can be traced back to the Sokoto Empire, an Islamic confederation that was based in northern Nigeria in the 19th century. The Hausa live in the mid-south region of Niger, where the population density is one of the highest in the country. Their area extends past the city of Filingué in the west, Zinder in the east, and from Tahoua to Niger's border with Nigeria. A small number can also be found as far north as the Aïr region.

Although the majority of the Nigerien Hausa are peasants, some of them are astute business people. They have created an economy based on cereal food crops, livestock, cash crops such as peanuts and cotton, and craft production. There are many excellent Hausa artisans in Niger, famous for their elaborate leatherwork. Their mobility and extensive business contacts have allowed their language to become the Nigerien national language. Hausa is understood and spoken by more than 60% of the population. Despite a common language and specific cultural heritage, the Hausa are composed of subgroups with their own states. They include the Arawa, Adarawa, Gobirawa, Katsinwa, Dorawa, Damagarawa, Tazarawa, Kouannawa, Kurfayawa, Damargawa, and Cangawa.

The Muslim Hausa society is characterized by a complex system of rank based on profession, wealth, and birth. Because wealth confers prestige, power, and status, occupational specializations are passed down from father to son.

A Hausa tailor making clothes. Hausa tailors are known for their intricate needlework.

THE SONGHAI-DJERMA

The Songhai and Djerma are different peoples who speak the same language. Because they share a common culture, other groups view them as one people. They are differentiated from each other by a slight difference in their local dialects and the theory of their origins before the 18th century. Forming almost 22% of the total population, the Songhai-Djerma are sedentary people who farm in the western part of the country near the Niger River. Apart from the late President Maïnassara, the first Hausa president of Niger, political power has remained in the hands of the Songhai-Djerma since Niger's independence.

The Djerma population is twice as large as the Songhai. They mainly live on the left bank of the Niger River, around the city of Dosso. Other Djerma live in Mali and Benin. Although their origin is still a question, they are known for their fighting agility and have helped their cousins, the Songhai, in numerous battles against the Tuareg and the Fulani.

The Songhai live on the right bank of the Niger River and in the Ayorou-Tillabéry region on the left bank. They also can be found in Mali, Benin, and Burkina Faso. The Songhai are descendants of the 15th-century Songhai Empire.

THE FULANI

The nomadic Fulani are a tall, fine-featured people who are scattered all over the Sahel and reside in almost all of Niger, except in the northeast oases. They also live in Nigeria, Cameroon, and other African countries. Another name for the Fulani is "Peul," a French word used by the French colonists. Numbering about 16 million in West Africa, they are of mixed African and Berber origins. They were also recorded as the first people to settle in the Senegambia region.

Since the last century, many Fulani have settled in the south. Most of them are engaged in agriculture. Others lead scholarly Islamic roles, while the rest are nomads in the north. Migrations to urban or semiurban regions have been getting more common in recent years as many Fulani gave up herding due to unpredictable crop harvests. Although the Fulani are the third largest group in Niger, forming about 8.5% of the total Nigerien population, they are not a majority in any region. The eight million Fulani in West Africa constitute the second largest ethnic group in the region, second only to the Hausa.

The Fulani, who speak Fulfuldé, are dispersed in various West African countries from Senegal to Chad. The close similarity of their language to the native language of Senegal indicates a possible origin in this West African country. It is believed that after adopting a new language in Senegal, they spread eastward by the 10th century and reached Nigeria by the 14th century.

Above: **A Fulani woman with tattooed lips.**

Opposite: **Songhai food vendors washing cans, which are used as food containers.**

By the 19th century, the Fulani established several kingdoms in Senegal and Cameroon. In a holy war in 1810, they conquered the Hausa states. However the Fulani were defeated by the British in the early 20th century.

Within the Fulani, the Bororo form a distinct subgroup, holding tightly to their ancient traditions. The Bororo live in the Dakoro-Tânout region. Most have preserved their animist beliefs, although some have converted to Islam. As lovers of beauty, they hold an annual *Gerewol* ("GER-e-wol") festival, a beauty contest for unmarried men. Although Bororo women pay great attention to their appearance, it is mainly the Bororo men who embellish themselves. Popular accessories include earrings, coins woven into an elaborate hairstyle, bead necklaces, and multicolored charms.

Watching the men dance in the *Gerewol* festival. These Bororo women will remove the brass trinkets after conceiving their second child.

THE KANOURI

The Hausa refer to the Kanouri as Beriberi. The Kanouri live east of the Hausa region and on the western side of Lake Chad. Their ancestors built the Kanem-Bornu Empire, which was known for its state organization. Like the Hausa and the Djerma-Songhai, the Kanouri are mostly farmers. They specialize in the preparation of salt, and many of them are excellent fishermen. Some are cattle herders. Through mixed marriages, they have blended with other groups.

The Kanouri are divided in subgroups: the Manga, the Dagora, the Mober, the Buduma, and the Kanumba. Besides Niger, the Kanouri live in Chad, Cameroon, and Nigeria.

A Kanouri woman checking the salt contents of a salt pan.

Jewelry is an important feature in the attire of the Tuareg women.

THE TUAREG

Descendants of the Berbers, the Tuaregs settled in the Aïr region as early as the seventh century, expanding their territory gradually to the entire Sahara region. Known as desert warriors, the Tuaregs are famous for their fighting skills. Today they are found in the Algerian, Nigerien, Malian, and Libyan portions of the Sahara, where they form about eight major groups.

In the past, the Tuaregs were known for capturing passing caravans and taking their prisoners as slaves. Today the Tuareg lead a nomadic life, although the droughts in the past decades have forced some to live permanently in cities such as Agadez.

The Tuaregs are divided into three major subgroups: the Kel Aïr, the Kel Azawak, and the Kel Geres. The Kel Aïr live in the Aïr region and the Damergou region. Most of them are gardeners and shopkeepers who travel on caravans from time to time. Most of the Kel Azawak are nomads, although a few pastorals can sometimes be found. The Kel Geres are pastorals and farmers.

AN OBJECT OF CURIOSITY: THE VEIL

One feature that has made the Tuareg an object of curiosity is the headdress and veil, worn by all adult Tuareg males. Despite its style variations, the basic veil, called the *tagelmust* ("tag-ERL-moost"), is a large piece of Sudanese cotton, measuring 59 to 158 inches (1.5 to 4 m) long by 10 to 20 inches (25 to 50 cm) wide. It can be made of several strips of cotton that the Tuareg wrap around the head to form a low turban. The veil rests on the nose and falls on the face down to the upper part of the chest. Only the eyes are revealed.

Once a Tuareg boy enters puberty, he will wear the veil in a family ceremony that marks his passage from adolescence to adulthood. From then on, he rarely goes unveiled, wearing it even while he is sleeping. The fold above the nose is frequently and slightly adjusted when he is in a group.

Although veiling is an ancient custom, its origins remain obscure. The veil holds an important place in Tuareg society, because it is a symbolic manifestation of the role status in Tuareg groups: the lower the veil is worn, the higher one's status.

The Tuareg society is matrilineal, and women have a prominent role. In contrast to the women in Arab and Muslim societies, Tuareg women are neither veiled nor secluded. Camp life is the Tuareg woman's domain, and she can own herds of animals and slaves. Women own the family property and manage the finances. They also play musical instruments and participate in organized musical performances.

The light-skinned Tuareg men are sometimes called "blue men." Except for their eyes, they wrap their entire body in indigo-dyed clothes as protection from the sandy winds and scorching sun, and the blue color rubs off onto their faces. At the end of the day, the men usually gather for their favorite pastime—the ceremonial sipping of tea next to a fire and talking about journeys in the desert.

A group of Toubou travelers with their camel caravans.

THE TOUBOU

A small number of Toubou live in dispersed settlements in areas north of Gouré, up to the Djado Plateau region. This tiny minority originated in the rocky region of Tibesti in Chad, where they number more than 30,000. There are also approximately 2,000 Toubou people living in Libya and Nigeria.

The Toubou are known for their quest for adventure and achievement and their love of war and guns. As highly independent individuals, they are divided into the Kesherda and the Wandalas. The Kesherda lead a seminomadic life and are excellent caravan travelers. They are also good cattle herders and hunters. The Wandalas lead sedentary lives.

ETHNIC MINORITIES

Besides the main ethnic groups, such as the Hausa and Fulani, there are a few small groups who live in the Republic of Niger. Some of them work for the main groups, while others form their own settlements. Niger's minorities include the Arabs and the Gourmantché, who are pastoralists. Together with the Toubou, they form about 1.2% of the Nigerien population. The Arabs live north of Tahoua and Nguigmi, dress like the Tuareg and speak their language, while the Gourmantché live on the right bank of the Niger River. The other minorities consist of black Africans from other countries, and a small number of Europeans. A large proportion of Europeans are French, descendants of the French colonists.

A black African doing household chores.

WOMEN IN SOCIETY

Although more than 13% of households are headed by women when their husbands leave the village to seek work in the cities or outside Niger, women's participation in the political arena is minimal. In 1995 the legislature only had one female member. A patriarchal system of values and the conservative interpretation of Islam have contributed to the exclusion of women from full participation in political and social life. As in most West African countries, discrimination against girls in education also exists in Niger. The result is a low literacy rate of 6.6% among females. The literacy rate of males is three times higher.

Among the women who receive an education, only a few reach high levels of public administration. If they do climb to the top, they encounter serious limitations. For example, there was public opposition to the nomination of a woman to the position of territorial administrator by former President Ousmane, forcing her to withdraw. At least two women, Aichatou Foumakoye and Aichatou Mindaoudou, have been nominated to the ministerial positions of social development and foreign affairs, respectively. In 1991, when educated women demanded a greater role in a

WOMEN IN A MALE-DOMINATED WORLD

Mariatou Mustapha has a commercial driving licence and is West Africa's only female commercial driver. A former bus driver in Niamey, Mariatou runs a driving school and shows concern for her female customers who do not get adequate service and help from men drivers. As a mother of two boys and three girls, and the second of four wives of a Hausa merchant, Mariatou is an exception to the Nigerien women's usual low status. Some African women drive their own cars, but none of them drive commercial vehicles. Although some own taxis or bush-taxis, they usually hire men to drive them. These businesses are not always profitable because their vehicles receive little care and collected fares are not always reported to them. Benefiting from her husband's liberal attitude, Mariatou's goal is to "show the men what a woman can do." She plans to establish a taxi line that will focus on the needs of women: transportation to dispensaries, clinics, and markets.

Although many Nigerien women are trying hard to improve their living conditions and social status, such efforts are slowed by obstacles, such as the rise of Muslim fundamentalism. In the city of Zinder, a pious population follows the clerics' call to stone and punish girls and women who do not wear headcloths. In addition, the women's center, newly built by the government, where girls were taught accounting, crafts, and typing, was burned down.

National Conference, they were met with hostility and physical violence from Islamic leaders.

In rural areas, women are actively involved in the continuous activity of survival, as well as in efforts to improve their children's health. Much of their time is spent hauling water, gathering firewood, doing the numerous household chores, and taking care of their offspring. Nigerien women have a high fertility rate, with an average of seven children each.

Several women's organizations, such as the Women Lawyers' Association in Niger (AFJN) and Democratic Rally of Women of Niger (RDFN), focus on women's issues. Unfortunately the AFJN suffers from low credibility, because its officers are full-time government employees who supported the January 1996 overthrow of the freely elected government of President Ousmane. The RDFN suffers from internal divisions stemming from personality differences among its leaders. Other associations lack financial support and face police intimidation. But not all of them are failures. Some private organizations attempt to oversee projects in rural areas that include educational work, the establishment of women's credit associations, health, and family planning. These projects have had some considerable success.

Opposite: **Nigerien girls on their way to the market to sell tomatoes.**

LIFESTYLE

DESPITE LIVING IN THE DESERT, the lifestyle of Nigeriens is very colorful and vibrant. More than 80% of Nigeriens live in rural areas, and their living habits vary according to the group's ethnicity, religion, profession, and residence. One characteristic held in common is the solidarity between members of the family and the community at large. Cooperation is an essential trait for survival. Especially in the rural areas, no one works alone; everyone has to chip in, in order to reap a bountiful harvest at the end of the agricultural year.

Urban centers offer people the opportunity to break away from the limits of ancient traditions, especially for those who come from less-developed areas. The social hierarchy of past empires— nobles, free men, and descendants of slaves—still exists today. It determines the interactions of the groups and an individual's profession.

Left: **Drawing water from a communal well.**

Opposite: **During the dry season when the rivers dry up, Nigeriens have to dig deep to find water.**

NOMADS

Nomads in Niger include mostly the Tuareg and the Fulani. The harsh and sometimes treacherous desert life requires strong ties between group members. To survive, everyone has to cooperate and work together for the good of the group.

A Tuareg nomadic group is usually composed of five noble families, five artisan families, and 15 slave families. When several clans form an alliance, the name of the alliance is prefixed with Kel. The largest Tuareg confederation is Kel Owey, which migrated to Niger around the 15th century. The leader of the clan is called *amrar* ("AHM-rahr"), which means old. The leader decides on the daily tasks of the camp and allocates activities to the artisans and herders. When a confederation of several clans unites, their leader is called *amenokal* ("ah-MEN-noh-kal").

Unlike the Tuareg groups, a less structured hierarchy exists among the Fulani. When an individual is born, he or she is categorized, based on kinship, age, sex, and generation. These remain important determinants of

Bororo Fulani nomads, who usually move around in groups.

existence, which the Fulani accept. Another factor that determines a person's status in Fulani society is the number of cattle the person owns and his success in rearing them.

The severe droughts in the 1970s and 1980s dealt a heavy blow to the nomads. They lost most of their herds, and the remaining people were forced to take on a sedentary life for which they were not prepared. Many sought refuge in neighboring countries.

More Tuaregs now lead a settled lifestyle, seeking employment in the mining areas.

TUAREG NOMAD GEAR

To survive in the desert, the Tuareg nomad must have necessary utensils and equipment. These include:

1. *Taoussit* ("TA-oh-seet"): A mat to sit or sleep on.
2. *Asaber* ("ah-SA-ber"): A mat used as a windscreen or to create a private space.
3. *Aghrik* ("ah-GREEK"): A leather bag that holds the family's belongings.
4. *Abayor* ("ah-BAR-yoor"): A goatskin, tanned with an acacia bark, which serves to hold fresh water. Its shape enables it to be easily carried by the animals.
5. *Tagelmust*: A long turban, which men wear on the head and use to cover their face.
6. *Alesho* ("ah-LEH-sho"): Indigo-colored cloth pieces sewn together and worn by the women like a scarf.

SOCIAL STRUCTURE

Niger's present population is the result of numerous migrations by different ethnic groups. Social structure mostly originated in the days of the trade caravans and wars. Most of these rankings are also prevalent in West Africa. As a consequence, a uniformity exists within the ethnic diversity of Niger. Each ethnic group is organized into family, clan, and confederations and is well adapted to both sedentary and nomadic lifestyles. In villages the elders, who are also keepers of oral tradition, maintain social organizations that determine the interactions between members of a social group, their social behavior, as well as interactions with other ethnic groups.

Ancient animist customs, coupled with Islamic traditions, continue to define the lives of the majority of the people. Rural lifestyles are now being affected by education-induced transformations. A greater number of people are also attracted to the more urbanized cities.

SOCIAL UNITS

In permanent settlements, the basic unit of Nigerien social life is the family. Nigeriens define themselves in terms of patrilineages, with all males and females descending from a

single male ancestor. Leaders are usually chosen from the oldest men in a family, and their duties include partitioning and allocating plots of land, resolving conflicts, arranging marriages, and officiating at ceremonies. Family members frequently consult them, and their advice is usually followed. Leadership is commonly passed down from father to son.

To increase national unity, the Nigerien government has urged people to strive toward creating a developing nation. In 1979 the authorities established a hierarchical structure of councils at the village, subregional (or arrondissement), regional (or départmental), and national levels. Except for village council members, the members of the other councils are either appointed or elected. Although the goal of the councils was to involve people in both economic and social development, many problems arose in implementing the policies, such as a lack of receptiveness, so results have not been satisfactory.

Above: **A tribal chief trying to resolve a conflict between his people and another village.**

Opposite: **A zebu pulling a pump, which draws water from a well, to irrigate the surrounding palm trees.**

63

A father and his two children. The boy on the left has a special haircut called the *zakara* ("ZAR-kah-rah"), which shows that the child is a male. The haircut resembles a rooster's comb.

FAMILY

Within the Hausa, intricate kinship relations develop through the male line, providing mutual support among the members in both rural and urban areas. The elders of a family intervene in every aspect of family life, such as promoting and arranging marriages for their juniors to strengthen family ties. Nonworking Hausa women stay in the family compound and only venture outside for medical treatment and family ceremonies. In general, relations between members of a group are cordial, although the closeness varies. Grandfathers develop joyful relationships with their grandchildren, while fathers rarely show affection toward their children.

Strong family ties among the Songhai group are illustrated by their large families: married sons live with their parents. The living compound is divided into a main room for the father, a room for each of his wives, and rooms for his sons and families. While the men go to work, Songhai women do household chores, such as fetching water, preparing meals, cleaning the house, and looking after the children.

For the rural Tuareg, family life surrounds the tent or compound, which bears the name of the woman owning the tent. Tuareg women enjoy prestige in their society. When a girl marries, her elderly female relatives will give her a tent as her dowry. The tent becomes a powerful element in the couple's relationship, as the husband risks eviction from the tent when spousal disagreements occur. Tuareg society differs from other Muslim societies in its cultural practices and beliefs. Music, dancing, and private courtship conversations are part of their lives, as all of these are considered expressions of joy and life.

In urban areas there are more nuclear families, as young married couples prefer to live by themselves. A lack of housing is a major problem for the rapidly increasing population, so living quarters often have to be shared with other family members, which leads to overcrowding. With a rise in the number of homeless, there are more thefts and social problems. Despite these deterrents, many young people still leave their villages for the conveniences of the cities.

Hausa polygamists are usually rich businessmen or respected elders.

MARRIAGE

Within each Nigerien community, marriage serves as a means of strengthening family ties and creating new ones. In Tuareg society, monogamy is the rule, but divorce is allowed. Tuareg parents do not arrange their children's marriage. Instead, playful courtship develops between young Tuareg boys and girls during community festivities.

According to Islam, Hausa and Songhai-Djerma men can have up to four wives. Divorce is allowed, but discouraged. In most villages parents arrange their daughter's marriage without her knowledge. The custom requires the man to pay a dowry to his future in-laws. Cases of arranged marriages between cousins often take place, and their failure causes rifts between the family members.

The rural customs of Hausa groups require that the oldest son of a family be polygamous, bestowing honor, respect, and consideration to his parents. His first wife's parents will offer their other daughters—the wife's younger sisters—to be the man's second, third, or fourth wife. Today, young, educated individuals oppose forced or polygamous marriages. Most of them defy their parent's wishes and take only one wife.

EDUCATION

Niger's system of education follows that of its former ruler, France. Although education in Niger is free, only a small fraction of children attend schools. In rural areas the distance to school is one major obstacle, since a junior high school is only available in the administrative center of an arrondissement, a high school in the administrative center of a département, and a university only in the capital city of Niamey. Before attending elementary school, children usually attend a school where they learn the *Koran* ("KOH-run"), the Muslim holy book, and the Islamic way of life.

Given their financial situation, many rural families do not send their children to school because they cannot afford to buy them stationery and books. In addition, the different ethnic groups view the establishment of schools with suspicion. As their children are taught a foreign language, parents are afraid that a social gap will be created between them, and that the school might "steal" their children from them. Thus they are not at all enthusiastic about sending their children to school. Some even go so far as to hide them from government officials. With recent education awareness campaigns targeted at the rural areas, parents are now reconsidering the option of sending their children to school. Many now realize the importance of education, as their agricultural efforts have often been thwarted by changing weather conditions.

To help rural families, the government has established elementary schools with room and board to house nomad children. One inconvenience of such boarding schools is the children's early separation from their parents. The children do not go home to visit during the school year.

Students studying in a Koranic school in Maradi.

Officially, eight years of free education is compulsory in Niger. Elementary education starts at age 7. At the end of secondary education students take the baccalaureate exam, which determines whether they can attend university. In 1995 the total number of registered students in elementary schools was approximately 400,000, compared to 80,000 in high schools and 5,000 in universities. Most of the teachers in elementary schools are Nigeriens, while professors in high schools and the university are French educators, teachers from other African countries, or US Peace Corps volunteers. There are also French schools, which teach only in French. There, instruction in the native languages is banned. Children learn French grammar, science, history, geography, drawing, and music.

Although the government grants scholarships to university students in Niamey, most of them come from well-to-do families and so do not need the money. Although antagonistic relations may exist among various ethnic groups, students from the different ethnic backgrounds bear no enmity toward one another. They treat each other with respect. With recent national budget cuts, job prospects for graduating students are poor, forcing them to complete their training in European or other African countries.

LITERACY

One of the major obstacles to the education program is the extremely low literacy rate. In 1995 only 13.6% of Nigeriens were literate, one of the lowest literacy rates in West Africa. Approximately 20.9% of men can read, compared to 6.6% of women.

The government has been unable to devise an education plan that embraces the country's varied language and cultural heritage and yet is still open to social and economic progress. If all the five major languages were taught, Nigeriens would not be able to communicate with one another while doing business. To tackle this problem and increase literacy, the government established vocational schools to train teachers in the Hausa and Songhai-Djerma languages. The teachers are then employed to teach reading and writing in local languages to adults in the rural areas. However, the uneducated portion of society questions the viability of studying in local languages, as there are no job opportunities for people who are trained in them.

Above: **A university student typing her assignment. Most university students are the first in their family, and sometimes the first in their village, to attend university.**

Opposite: **A teacher inscribing verses from the *Koran* on a wooden tablet.**

In Koranic schools, students are taught the entire Koran, *the Muslim holy book, before advancing to the next level, which is learning a second language.*

Recently the failings of the education system have forced some people to enroll in *Koranic* schools, which excel in teaching verse reciting. To expand Islam into Sub-Saharan Africa, Saudi Arabia and Libya started to construct several Islamic centers. In 1987 Saudi Arabia built an Islamic university in Niger. It was the first Islamic university in West Africa. However, after a few years of operation, it was closed following political disagreement between the Saudi and Nigerien governments.

STUDENT MOVEMENTS

The student movement remains at the forefront of the political movement for social change in Niger. During the military rule of Kountché, students and trade unions led the popular strike that brought down the government. During the 1989–90 school year, strikes and demonstrations for better equipment and improved facilities forced the national university to declare that year "a white year:" the academic year was canceled, and students had to repeat that year. In addition, the government's decision to send military troops to quell the student demonstrations resulted in many student deaths and injuries on the Kennedy Bridge in Niamey on February 9, 1990. In other cities students were beaten and arrested, then tortured. Because many of the victims were children of high government officials, protests spread quickly, and multiparty elections were demanded. As a result, the constitution was suspended, the government dissolved, and a transitional government ruled until the first multiparty elections of 1993.

The student movement is also strong among Nigerien students who study in other African countries, such as Benin, Algeria, and Tunisia, where they frequently demonstrate, sometimes taking over the Nigerien embassies when their scholarships are not paid.

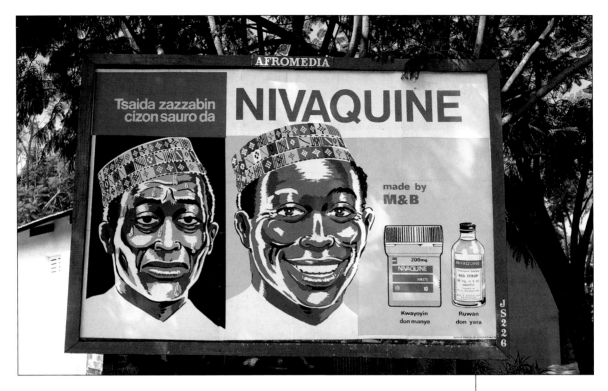

HEALTH

Healthcare facilities in Niger are inadequate, and about half of the population does not have access to health services. The principal causes of death are illnesses caused by parasites, especially malaria. Niger falls within the African meningitis belt with outbreaks taking place between the months of December and June. In 1998 several thousand cases of meningitis were reported throughout the country, including Zinder, where close to 1,000 cases occurred.

The government's health program includes eradication of diseases in rural areas and health education. Children are given vaccinations against smallpox and measles. Diseases such as tuberculosis, malaria, trachoma, and leprosy remain endemic and continue to pose serious health problems. Major causes of these diseases spreading are the lack of running water and sewage systems. To alleviate these health problems, some rural Nigeriens seek the help of local medicine men, who usually blame the illness on witchcraft and evil spirits.

An advertisement showing the benefits of an anti-malaria medicine. With a life expectancy of 44 years in 1994, the rural population suffers from a lack of access to hospitals and healthcare in general. In the same year, the infant mortality was 111 per 1,000, one of the highest figures in West Africa.

71

RELIGION

ISLAM HAS PLAYED A VITAL ROLE in uniting the ethnic mosaic of Niger, but problems are surfacing as the rising fundamentalist movement attempts to use religious teachings to gain power. In Zinder, where they are a majority, Muslim fundamentalists have forced the government to forbid girls from wearing skirts. They also intimidate members of non-government organizations who provide health education to women.

Although about 80% of the Nigerien population are Sunni Muslims, many Nigeriens remain attached to their animist beliefs and practice both beliefs. Some groups still hold on very strongly to their traditional practices. The Bororo Fulani and the Azna Hausa practice only their ancient cult religions. About 50,000 Nigeriens are Christians. Although many missions are found scattered throughout the country, only a small fraction of Nigeriens have converted.

Left: **It does not matter where a Muslim is, as long as he or she can find a quiet place to pray. Here, a traveling Muslim stops his vehicle in the middle of nowhere for his noon prayers.**

Opposite: **A mosque in Maradi.**

INTERPRETATION OF RELIGION

To Nigeriens, religion provides a theoretical interpretation of the world. It can predict and control worldly events and supply answers to their problems. They believe that puzzling occurrences, such as sickness, or financial success or demise, require explanations that religion can provide, and that order and regularity is the main objective of human interactions. Certain aspects of a person's life are also thought to be controlled by invisible natural forces or spirits, whose anger can be allayed or prevented by specific gifts and sacrifices.

In Niger, faith in more than one religion is widespread among the population. Many Muslims practice pagan and animist customs and hold ancient ceremonies and rituals, which are against the teachings of Islam. Resorting to ancestral beliefs, witchcraft and ritual spirit cults seem to be the result of the people's inability to find in the main religions answers to the worldly events that affect their lives. Many Nigeriens convert to Islam and Christianity because their leaders have converted, and they feel it is necessary to follow suit.

Above: **Muslims gather outside a mosque for noon prayers. Devout Muslims have to pray five times a day.**

Opposite: **A modern mosque in Niamey.**

INTRODUCTION OF ISLAM

One of the earliest Muslim groups settled in Kanem, on the Chad frontier, after the fall of the Kharedjite rebellion in A.D. 947. By the 11th century, other Muslim groups, as well as merchants, scholars, nomads, and craftsmen, had settled in the area. Trade relations soon developed between Kanem and the Muslim states of North Africa.

Although the Muslim religion suggested the freeing of slaves, trade caravans still brought them across Niger to Egypt and the Fezzan in Libya and to Egypt. Within the country, the social structure saw the creation of a slave class and that of slave owners. The people's ensuing economic prosperity increased the influx of merchants, Muslim scholars, and smiths. Leaders of local clans turned into powerful rulers. They sought the help of Muslim scholars to expand their rule to adjacent regions, pitting one ethnic group against another. In one example in the 19th century, the Fulani waged a war against enemies of Islam and occupied Hausa states.

Several orders of Sunni Muslims are predominant in Niger. The Tidjaniya, the largest maraboutic fraternity, has been the most popular among the Kanouri and the Songhai-Djerma since the 1920s. It was first established near Laghouat, Algeria, and during the French occupation, spread south. Despite an initial opposition to French occupation of Niger, the order later reached a compromise with the French authorities from which it won favors. In contrast, the Sanussiya, a Sunni Sufi order, galvanized and spearheaded the Tuareg and Toubou groups' uprising against the French, who conducted harsh reprisals in return.

Muslims congregating at a mosque on Friday.

ISLAM IN NIGER TODAY

Among African nations, Niger sends the fewest Muslim pilgrims to Mecca, the Muslim holy site. Mecca is the birthplace of the prophet Mohammed, whom Muslims believe was the last messenger of God. Muslims are taught that besides the *Koran* ("KOH-run"), the Muslim holy book, Mohammed's sayings are the next most accurate revelations of their God, Allah.

Niger's constitution separates religion and state but does not stop government officials from taking part in public religious ceremonies. Wealthier Muslim men confine their wives to their house compounds, but the women do not wear the veil or the *hidjab* ("hee-JAB"), a piece of cloth covering their body, as do many Muslim women. The less wealthy women have to work, and so do not stay in the house all day.

Unlike North African states, where aggressive fundamentalist movements have resulted in civil war, for example in Algeria, Niger has been able to achieve a compromise between its traditional customs and the Muslim religion. Nigeriens are happy to maintain this harmonious relationship.

CHRISTIANITY

In 1998 there were about 50,000 Nigerien Christians. Christianity remains the religion of the towns, particularly Niamey. Many Christians are Europeans and non-Nigerien Africans who live in Niger. The main denominations are Roman Catholic and Protestant. There are 12 Roman Catholic mission centers, one diocese, and 13 Protestant mission centers.

Early missionary work in West Africa from the 15th to the 19th centuries focused on the communities on the Atlantic coast and countries south of Niger. The first Catholic mission in Niger was established in 1931 by Bishop Steinmetz of Upper Volta. In the 1940s African Missions of Lyon, known as the Fathers of Lyon, started their work in the city of Zinder. Unlike the pre-colonial Muslim missionaries and rulers in Niger who legitimized polygamy and traded slaves, Christian missionary workers insisted that Nigeriens become monogamous, eliminate superstition, and that slaves be freed. Christians focused their efforts on building religious schools and improving public health facilities and dispensaries to attract converts.

Christians attending church on Sunday.

THE BORI CULT

Although the main religion is Islam, many Nigeriens still practice traditional cult rituals to seek relief from sicknesses or to explain unfortunate occurrences. These practices include the *yenendi* ("yay-NAN-dee"), an ancient ritual to summon rain, sacrifices to appease or feed the gods, and sanctification of animals such as snakes, which followers believe look after the safety of their families and community as a whole.

The *Bori* ("BOH-ree"), meaning "spirit," is a spiritual cult of Niger that is practiced by a Hausa group called the Azna. The Azna are descendants of the Hausa who were chased out of the Aïr regions by the Tuaregs and are one of the few groups who still retain their traditional rites.

The *Bori* ritual is a ceremony organized to call on the almighty gods to intervene directly in worldly events and human affairs by possessing the body of an initiated woman or girl. Members of the cult include women from many roles in the rural society. They usually pray to the gods to drive away sickness and infertility.

The initiation rites are a monthly event. In the presence of the chiefs, *serkin* ("SIR-kin")

Bori, the women to be initiated are brought forward by the *Bori* queen, who is called *magajiya* ("mah-GAH-jee-yah"). The chiefs are the ones who officiate at the ceremony. The women start the ritual by dancing and continuing until they are in a frenzied trance. The ritual ends when the woman collapses on the ground, indicating that she is finally a *Bori*—and possessed by a spirit.

In areas such as Maradi and Niamey, the ritual was so widespread and the cult influence so strong that the political support of the *Bori* queens was much sought after in the early days of independence. The leadership of the *Bori* queens was instrumental in the creation of several women's organizations, such the Union of Nigerien Women.

Opposite: **A young Nigerien wearing a charm. *Bori* followers believe charms can ward off evil spirits.**

Below: **Maradi is one region where *Bori* rituals are common.**

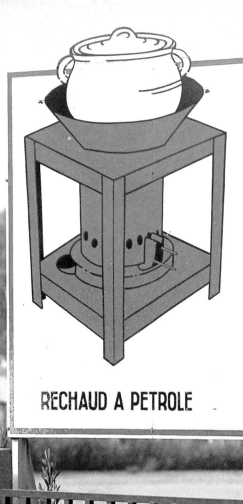

★ PRATIQUE

★ PAR TOUS LES TEMPS

★ ECONOMIQUE

★ TOUS LES PLATS

 TCHIP
La Cuisine 4 Etoiles

RECHAUD A PETROLE

LANGUAGE

NIGER HAS THREE MAIN CULTURES: African, Muslim, and French. Within this diverse heritage, language is the primary element that separates Nigeriens into several different groups. Until France's occupation of the country, the principal languages were Songhai, Hausa, and Tamasheqt, and smaller communities continued to speak a variety of dialects. During the French occupation, a few schools that taught only French were constructed in the main cities, and the French-speaking people became an elite group.

Today, as Niger's official language, French is the language of instruction in schools and higher institutions. It is also the language used in the administration, industry, and finance. Most of the media, including television and radio broadcasts, and newspapers use French. However, only a minority of the population speaks French.

Left: **A school in Zinder. The students are learning French.**

Opposite: **A sign in French, the official language of Niger.**

LANGUAGE

Nigeriens generally speak two or three languages. Native languages allow for interactions within and outside ethnic groups. The French language allows Nigeriens to communicate with the rest of the world. Nigeriens also use Arabic to recite verses of the *Koran*.

There are at least 21 known languages and dialects in Niger, some of which are spoken by as few as 3,000 individuals. Each ethnic group speaks its own language, but Hausa has become the language for trade in most of Niger. Recently, pilot schools have started to teach the main native languages, Hausa and Songhai-Djerma. A number of French-Arabic schools, financed by the fundamentalist movement in the major urban areas, conduct two-thirds of their lessons in Arabic.

Koranic students in a courtyard. The wooden slates they are holding contain Koranic verses.

HAUSA

Nomads bargaining in Hausa.

Hausa is the native language of about half the Nigerien population. The language belongs to the Chadic branch of the Afro-Asiatic language family. In the regions where it is spoken, Hausa has a uniform vocabulary and structure that make its variations mutually comprehensible.

At the time of the colonial conquest, people began to use the Roman script as a written form of the Hausa language. The first documents in Romanized form dated from the early 1930s and were introduced by the British administration. The second writing system is called *Ajami* ("ah-JAH-mee"), which means "non-Arab" or "foreigner" in Arabic. *Ajami* uses the Arabic system of writing with minor adaptations for particular Hausa sounds. At the beginning of the 19th century, *Ajami* allowed learned, religious people to write Islamic poetry in praise of the prophet Mohammed and his followers and to extol Islamic doctrine. Much of Hausa writing today, however, uses Romanized characters for transcription, similar to the Hausa literature printed in Nigeria.

SONGHAI-DJERMA

The language used by the Songhai-Djerma is the second most spoken native language. It is also used in Mali, northern Burkina Faso, and Benin. The Djerma language belongs to the Songhai family of languages in Mali, and the Songhai language belongs to the Nilo-Saharan group of the Afro-Asiatic family of languages. Although Djerma is a dialect of Songhai, the Songhai people of Niger understand Djerma. The differences between the two are subtle, and people who are not well-versed in them can hardly tell them apart. When combined, the Songhai-Djerma population in Niger number about 2.5 million.

Songhai-Djerma and Hausa are considered the second languages of Niger. Other ethnic groups learn either Hausa or Songhai-Djerma as required by their environment. These languages provide a tool of communication among the ethnic groups, including the Fulani, Tuareg, Kanouri, Toubou, Gourmanché, and other minorities, in markets and workplaces.

FULFULDÉ

The language of the Fulani is called Fulfuldé and is sometimes referred to as Fula or Pulaar. It is classified as a Northern Atlantic branch of the Niger-Congo family of languages. It is spoken by about 16 million people spread across almost all the countries of West Africa. Despite the extremely large region they inhabit, their dialects only differ slightly.

The Fulani use two systems of transcription in their language: the *Ajami*, with slight modification for special Fulfuldé sounds, and Latin characters modified for special consonant sounds. The Fulfuldé language has a particular system of word derivation from verb forms, allowing the root verb to be at the center of the Fulfuldé lexicon.

The older Fulani can only speak Fulfuldé.

Two Tuareg men reading a book in the Tifinagh alphabet.

TAMASHEQT

The language of the Tuareg is Tamasheqt, which has its own alphabet called Tifinagh ("tee-FEE-nahr"). Tamasheqt is one of the Amazigh or Berber languages found in North Africa that belong to the Afro-Asiatic family. As a matriarchal society, Tuareg women are responsible for passing on to their children the language of their ancestors and its transcription. Their duties include teaching the young the Tifinagh alphabet, which recently has become more popular with the advent of a strong movement to revive the Berber culture and language in Morocco and Algeria. Until recently, Tamasheqt was limited to poetry and love messages. It is now used in more aspects of the Tuaregs' lives. During their recent uprising, the Tuareg demanded political autonomy and greater control of their cultural and language heritage.

OTHER LANGUAGES

There are other languages and dialects used by the smaller ethnic groups. The Kanouri and the Toubou languages belong to the Nilo-Saharan family, while Gourmanchéma, the language of the Gourmantché, belongs to the Niger-Congo family. The Kanouri people in Niger use the *Ajami* transcription to write Kanouri . The Toubou language is spoken by the Toubou people, who also speak Arabic.

LANGUAGE AND THE STATE

During its occupation of Niger, France did not try to impose the French language on Nigeriens. Only a limited number of schools were built. After independence, despite the government's efforts to improve literacy, only one-fifth of Niger's population spoke fluent French. Beyond the urban areas, fluency in French is rare today.

Since independence, the Nigerien government has retained French as the official language, while actively promoting the native languages. The government has included news in the native languages in television broadcasts. The only television station in Niger broadcasts daily news in Hausa and Djerma in between French programs, and once a week, it broadcasts news in Tamasheqt, Fulfuldé, Kanouri and Toubou, Gourmanchéma, and Arabic. The few radio stations in Niger also have to provide slots for news in the native languages.

During a national conference in July 1991, a proposal to make Hausa the official language of Niger failed as the other major ethnic groups opposed it, especially the politically powerful Songhai-Djerma and Tuareg groups. As a result, the government has decided not to have one definite language or fixed education program but to recognize the languages of the five major ethnic groups.

There are half a million speakers of Kanouri in Niger today.

THE MEDIA

In 1999 the newspapers available in Niger were *Le Sahel*, a government-owned newspaper published daily in Niamey, and *Sahel Dimanche*, a weekend newspaper; and a number of independent newspapers, such as *Alternative, Anfani, Démocrate, Le Républicain, and La Tribune du Peuple.* Niger has only one state-owned television channel and four privately-owned radio stations, namely Radio Anfani, R & M, Souda, and Ténéré F.M.

THE NEW PRESS LAW OF 1997

The press law of 1997 treats any criticism of or relaying of information unfavorable to those in power as a felony. Although the government indicated that the new law will "clean up the newspaper profession," radio owners, newspaper publishers, and democratic political parties have accused the government of trying to stifle the private media, which already suffers from political pressure and economic malaise.

PRESS FREEDOM AWARD

Grémah Boucar, director of the independent radio station Radio Anfani and publisher of the bimonthly news magazine *Anfani* received the International Freedom Award of the Committee to Protect Journalists on November 24, 1998, in New York. Boucar and Radio Anfani were the target of attacks by military troops during General Maïnassara's rule. Boucar's radio station was shut down in 1996 and ransacked by military troops in 1997 because of his criticism of the government's actions and his opposition to press censorship. Boucar and some Radio Anfani journalists have been taken into custody several times. Thirty-nine-year-old broadcaster Boucar is an example of Africa's emerging independent broadcasters and journalists who oppose Africa's authoritarian and intolerant governments despite threats from the authorities.

Radio Anfani was launched in 1994 during the administration of Niger's first democratically elected president, Mahamane Ousmane. The radio station quickly attracted a large Nigerien audience. While a number of journalists covered local news, Radio Anfani also rebroadcast news programs from the Voice of America, the British Broadcasting Service, and Radio Deutsche Welle.

Despite the low literacy rate of the population, Niger's government has suppressed freedom of the press for many years, primarily targeting the country's independent media. In an attempt to intimidate the journalists and writers, the government has resorted to ordering newspaper directors to pay huge fines or face confiscation of their printing presses. Journalists who do not hold an official press card issued by the government are banned. Bureaucratic policies require a journalist to have five years of field experience to obtain an official press card. If they breach any of the press laws, they will face two to five years of imprisonment or be required to pay fines ranging from $340 to $8,600. Radio stations are not spared from these restrictions. Independent radio stations are told not to rebroadcast foreign news programs on the basis that foreign broadcasts do not conform to Niger's press code.

Two publishers, one from *La Tribune du Peuple*, and the other from *Le Citoyen*, were found guilty of defamation after they published reports of drug smuggling and passport fraud allegedly involving Niger's consul in Saudi Arabia. Moussa Tchangari, the editor of the weekly newspaper, *Alternative*, was sentenced to three months in prison and fined $85 for publishing correspondence between the prime minister's office and the minister of higher education and reporting on corruption and nepotism.

ARTS

ART PLAYS AN IMPORTANT ROLE IN NIGER'S ECONOMY. Artisans in each ethnic group excel in making one or two types of artifacts, depending on their living environment and way of life. Pottery making, particularly earthenware water jars, is the forte of Djerma women. The Songhai make blankets and weave mats. Tuareg artisans make excellent silver jewelry with elaborate motifs, leatherwork with exquisite designs, as well as sculpt wood and make utensils, tent equipment, and saddles. Fulani women are adept at engraving calabashes, weaving, and basketry.

Although Nigerien arts have retained their traditional forms, modern Nigerien painters have drawn inspiration from Western and Muslim styles and integrated them in their paintings. Exhibitions of Nigerien art are usually held in the Niger Museum, which is located in Niamey. Built in 1958, the musuem exhibits many artifacts and works of art by the different ethnic groups.

Most artists are self-taught, as there are few art schools in Niger. To cultivate more local talent and preserve the country's artistic and cultural heritage, the Niger Museum has started an apprenticeship program.

Left: **A morning market in Niger. To Nigeriens, these baskets, which are woven by hand, serve a practical purpose rather than an aesthetic one.**

Opposite: **A Nigerien mother and her two children carry pots of water on their heads.**

Hausa minstrels performing at a Ramadan feast. Like their Tuareg counterparts, the Hausa love music.

MUSIC AND THE TUAREG

Playing music and singing are important elements in any Nigerien social event. Music is used to celebrate human events, such as births, weddings, circumcisions, and religious holidays. The musicians and their audiences share in a creative performance, to experience a communal activity, and to express feelings of comraderie.

As guardians of traditions and customs in the Tuareg society, women have greatly contributed to the Tuareg cultural heritage. As a result, music is not a man's sole privilege; women play music as well, although their styles differ. Women play most traditional instruments, except for flutes.

The women's musical styles include the *tindé* ("TUHN-day") and the *ezelé* ("ay-ZAY-lay"). The *tindé* is the most common musical rhythm in Niger. It is created by a drumlike instrument called a *tindé* that is made with a mortar with goatskin stretched across its opening. In the *tindé* performance, the player also sings to the rhythm she makes with the instrument. *Ezelé* is a dance music played to accompany male dancers.

Artisans making shoes.

LEATHERWORK AND JEWELRY

Tuareg artisans, called *inadan* ("EEN-ah-dan"), are excellent craftspeople, making silver jewelry, saddles, camel bags, tools, utensils, and talismans. They also specialize in leather products, such as traditional money purses and shoes. Leather shoes are made from the raw hide for protection from scorpions, thorns, and sand fleas. The soles must be wide to allow support on the fine sand. Decorative patterns are intricate, and when dyed-leather is used, these items become art pieces that can be worn only at special occasions. Female *inadan* also sew water containers from goatskins. Apart from leather, ladles are embroidered with dyed wool. From the Saharan scrub and trees, artisans make ladles, carve bowls, and construct beds.

Tuareg artisans create a wide range of rings, anklets, and amulets. But the most well-known jewelry item is the Agadez silver cross, called a *teneghelt* ("te-NER-gelt"), sometimes referred to as the Cross of the South (of Europe). Several designs exist, each pattern representing a clan or confederation. In Niger nearly every city is represented by its silver cross.

HAUSA FOLKLORE

With a low literacy rate, Niger's folklore is best preserved in the form of oral tales, legends, and proverbs. Riddles, poetry, and the lyrics of old songs also contain some age-old stories. The literature of the Hausa people is vast and varied. As the Hausa converted to Islam, they also began to transcribe poetry in *Ajami* script. The main characters in a Hausa folk tale can be an animal, a man, a woman, a hero, or a villain. All folk tales attempt to highlight for the audience some traditional values and morals of their culture. Other tales include legends, which can be historical accounts of former rulers or stories of spirits. The Hausa believe in the presence of powerful spirits that intervene in their daily lives.

Storytelling is not confined to the home. Here, a mother recites an old Hausa tale to her son.

WALL DECORATION

The Hausa are a very creative people, and their art is visible in their houses.
To add sparkle to the dull earthy tones of their homes, the Hausa paint
colorful motifs on the exterior walls. The patterns used are greatly
influenced by Islamic and African styles. Original African motifs underline
much of the decoration found in Hausa textile embroidery and wall
decorations. Elaborate and intricate decorative patterns are also part of
Hausa architecture. Early geometric mud decorations mainly adorn doors
and other openings, and they were probably the result of old charms used
to ward off evil intruders. Later, the decoration expanded to include
entire walls.

GRIOTS

Africa's oral traditions can be compared to the abundant libraries in Western countries. To retain this oral tradition, every ethnic group has *griots* ("GREE-yaws"), who are masters of the spoken word. During cultural celebrations in villages and cities, the eloquent *griots* will share with their audience many centuries-old folktales, stories, proverbs, poetry, legends, riddles, and historical epics. Their moving tales have captivated Western researchers interested in the cultural history of Niger and West Africa. These scholars have recently started to concentrate on learning more about the rich Nigerien customs and traditions, as well as their literature, history, sociology, and anthropology.

The Sultan of Zinder with his councillors at his palace. Among his advisors is a *griot*.

As a poet, storyteller, and musician, the *griot* is a walking encyclopedia for his people. He knows all the historical and cultural facts about his people, community, and country. He is the transmitter of a wealth of knowledge from one generation to another. Sometimes he is an official member of the royal court of a local chief, living permanently among his community. In some villages he lives apart from the local community but is allowed to speak freely. A *griot* can also be employed to work in a village or a city. He is hired for family celebrations and electoral campaigns. There are *griots* in all the Songhai-Djerma, Hausa, and Kanouri ethnic groups.

The *griot* is both feared and respected in Nigerien society. According to African wisdom, words are God's gift to a *griot*. They are considered sacred, and Nigeriens believe they contain magical powers that the *griot* can summon in ritual chants and rhythmic incantations to feed nature's spirits and forces. A *griot* may also extol the glories of powerful rulers or scoff at past incidents. Some *griots* have special relationships with their masters, acting as advisors. In the past, during wars, the *griots* would accompany their masters, usually rulers of a region, to battlefields so that they could tell stories to boost the boldness and strength of the soldiers.

JELIBA THE GREAT GRIOT

Known as Jeliba the Great *Griot*, Jibo Baje still narrates the epics of Africa accompanied by the warm music of his lute. To learn more about his country's traditions and to better preserve its heritage, Jeliba has expanded his sources and studied the different versions of the epics. In his search, he has traveled beyond Niger to consult elders. Having already benefited from his traditional teaching, Jeliba now uses his sharp voice and his music to sing the common heritage and culture of Niger, reminding his audience of bygone days.

Books on display in a bookshop.

LITERATURE

Currently, Nigerien authors publish very few books in their own language. Until recent decades, the country's culture was conveyed orally from one generation to another. During family gatherings, the older folks would impart to the young their knowledge of the history and traditions of Niger and their ethnic group, as well their own experiences.

As the African saying goes "An old man who dies is a library that burns." Many Nigeriens are starting to realize the historical disconnection that can result from the lack of writing. This accounts for the increase in Nigerien literature in French that can be found today. The authors record the rich oral traditions and customs, giving the words of older generations an everlasting life span.

The first Nigerien to ever publish a book before independence was Ibrahim Issa. He published *Les Grandes Eaux Noires* (The Large Black Waters). His most popular work is a book of poetry called *La Vie et Ses Faceties* (Life and its Jokes) that contains the exploits of great African leaders, such as Samory, Issa Korombey, Béhanzin, and Lumumba. It is written in the style of an African traveling poet and musician. Another writer is the former president of the National Assembly, Boubou Hama, who died in 1983. Born in 1906, he was the author of more than 40 books, including important works on ancient empires, as well as traditional folktales and essays. In 1970 he was awarded the Grand Prix Littéraire de l'Afrique Noire, the great literary prize of Sub-Sahara Africa, for his autobiography *Kotia Nima*.

ALPHADI: AN AFRICAN FASHION DESIGNER IN PARIS

Born to a Tuareg father from Timbuktu in Mali and a Tuareg mother from Niger, Seidnaly Alphadi is considered the representative of new African fashion. He skillfully combines the exotic and traditional colors and styles of Africa to attract Western taste. He is one of the few fashion designers from Africa whose style has penetrated the international fashion scene in Paris and New York.

Even though he was born with talent, Alphadi worked very hard to become what he is today. While preparing for a doctorate in tourism from a school in Paris, he took evening classes in fashion and design, and worked as a model for Giorgio Armani. On his return to Niger, he held the position of Director of Tourism Promotion but resigned soon after. He headed for Paris and New York to complete his training in fashion design. In 1986 he introduced his first collection and has since won countless fashion prizes and medals.

Alphadi's ambition is for his fashion to be seen by the world and to be understood in Africa. He also wants to promote communication between African fashion designers, Western fashion promoters, and African businessmen. He believes there are other potential areas for expansion, such silver jewelry making and leather crafts. They would create more jobs in the textile, leather, and cosmetic industries.

There exists no Nigerien literature in English.

MODERN MUSIC AND ART

Even though Nigeriens are very interested in traditional art, they do not condemn modern art forms. On the contrary, contemporary art is embraced by younger Nigeriens. In Niamey, groups of young singers, for instance the group Black-Dapss, perform Nigerien rap music, using music to convey messages about social problems, such as drugs and AIDS. The freelance theater company Les Tréteaux du Niger, formed in 1994, has been innovative. Since Nigeriens do not attend plays, the freelance comedians decided to seek the public wherever they may be. Their repertoire includes six original creations adapted from Molière, Corneille, and Shakespeare, and they have performed more than 250 times in towns and villages in Niger, Africa, and Europe. Rissa Ixa is a Tuareg painter born in Ayorou. His paintings are records of the vanishing Tuareg life. His goal is to preserve cultural heritage by educating society.

LEISURE

NIGERIENS ARE A VERY SOCIABLE PEOPLE. Their leisure is centered around events that bring together friends, family, or the community. The majority of Nigeriens like to partake in social events that define their ethnic identity. Traditional gatherings, such as spirit ceremonies, attract large public crowds, as they represent an ancient heritage. Communal gathering places, including markets, are not only a place for daily grocery shopping but are also a busy and lively arena where, among other things, friends and associates meet, news is spread, and the latest fashion trends are learned.

Besides traditional activities, modern sports, such as wrestling and soccer, have caught on in Niger. Many people now enjoy watching matches either live or on television. City dwellers have also adopted several Western-style leisure activities. Going to the movies is quickly becoming popular.

Left: **Children playing blind man's bluff.**

Opposite: **A Nigerien village chief resting outside his house.**

SPORTS

Traditional wrestling is a popular sport. Many people flock to the championship games held by the Ministry of Sports and Culture. Long-distance running has also gained some fans since three Nigeriens— Gabirou Dan Mallan, Issoufou Ouseini, and the 1996-winner Moussa Yeli—took top positions in the 11th 13-mile (21-km) marathon in Abidjan, Côte d'Ivoire, in 1998.

The Nigerien government has taken an active role in the promotion of sports in the country. So far, they have supported sports organizations and organized games, promoted traditional sports, and formed teams to take part in international games. Their commendable efforts have paid off.

In 1972 Nigerien lightweight boxer Issaka Daboré won the bronze medal at the Olympic Games in Munich. He also won several medals in various African competitions.

Among modern sports, soccer is the preferred sport of Nigeriens, offering a source of entertainment for men and young boys. It has become the most popular sport in Niger because of the bonding that results from the various African and World Cup competitions that attract millions of spectators. With a soccer league that organizes tournaments for teams from different regions, Niger is able to participate with other African countries on a regular basis. In February 1999 the youth and sports ministers of Francophone countries voted to hold the fifth Francophone Games in 2005 in Niger.

Players taking part in a soccer tournament.

A cinema in Niamey. Nigerien moviegoers do not watch a movie in silence. The atmosphere is lively, with clapping and laughing, and people will comment on the movie during the viewing.

ENTERTAINMENT

Household electronic equipment has brought dramatic changes to Nigerien leisure. Many urban dwellers now own television sets, video cassette recorders, and stereos. American television series, such as *Dynasty* and *Colombo,* broadcast on Nigerien television are very popular among English-speaking Nigeriens. Urban teenagers also enjoy watching Hindi dramas and karate action movies.

Every large city has an outdoor cinema where Nigeriens can enjoy the latest movies. In Niamey, movie festivals, conferences, and art shows are held at the Oumarou Ganda Cultural Center or the French Cultural Center.

DARA

Both young and old men play *dara* ("da-RAH"), a game similar to checkers. There are usually two players. Pits of the dum-dum tree fruit are used as pieces. To play, rows and columns of holes are made in the sand. One player puts the pits in his share of holes, while his adversary uses small millet twigs in his holes. The objective is for each player to move his pieces to the farthest row of holes.

SHARRO

Sharro ("SHAR-raw") is a sport-like activity practiced by pastoral Fulani youngsters when they enter manhood. It is an endurance and bravery test and is performed by two opponents. According to his partner's age and category, the giver violently hits his partner with a tree twig or a stick a certain number of times. His partner, the receiver, must endure the pain, pretending not to be hurt. He must also smile at the audience to prove his excellent control over pain. A year after, the roles are reversed. The competition can continue for many years.

Boys playing with their homemade cart.

Sharro has many categories, ranging from young to old. Because it is a dangerous game, and people have been badly injured, the Nigerien government has forbidden the game. Althought it is not practiced at public festivals and ceremonies in the towns anymore, some people still practice it secretly outside the villages.

FESTIVALS

NIGERIENS LOVE AN EXCUSE to meet friends and family to eat and enjoy themselves, so the numerous festivals in Niger provide them with many opportunities to gather for a feast. Whether the holidays are religious or secular, there is always plenty to eat.

MUSLIM HOLIDAYS

Muslim religious holidays include Eid al-Fitr and Eid al-Adha. Celebrations follow the lunar calendar and consequently are held at different dates every year. With the Muslim year being 11 days shorter than the year of the Gregorian calendar, it takes about 33 years for the holy month of Ramadan to fall in the same month again. During Ramadan, Muslims fast from sunrise to sunset, abstaining from eating, drinking, and smoking.

Left: **A Hausa minstrel and dancing women celebrate the *Tabaski* ("tah-BAH-skee"), a Muslim festival.**

Opposite: **Minstrels lead a Hausa procession from the mosque.**

Young Hausa women wearing new clothes for Eid al-Adha. Besides getting new clothes for this festival, children also receive money and gifts from their parents and relatives. Tuareg boys may get a camel from their uncles, while Tuareg girls may get small pieces of jewelry.

Eid al-Fitr, or the Feast of Eating, marks the end of Ramadan and is celebrated with family and friends. On this day, the men wake up early in the morning to gather in the mosque for prayers. After prayers, relatives and friends visit one another, and children are given money and treats. A large feast is served for lunch.

Eid al-Adha, or the Feast of the Sacrifice, is known in Niger as *Tabaski*. It commemorates the prophet Abraham's willingness to sacrifice his son and is the highlight for those who have completed the *hajj* ("HAHJ"). The *hajj* is a pilgrimage to the holy city of Mecca in Saudi Arabia.

For the male Muslims, Eid al-Adha starts with a morning prayer, led by an *imam* ("EE-mahm"), a Muslim spiritual leader, at the mosque. At the end of the prayers, the *imam* will slaughter a ram, a signal to the followers that they can go ahead and slaughter their own rams. The sacrifice of a ram symbolizes the giving of oneself to Allah. The meat is usually distributed to friends, neighbors, and poor people. During this time, Muslims are reminded to be compassionate and help the poor and needy.

Muslims praying outside
the Great Mosque during
the Bianou festival.

THE BIANOU FESTIVAL

To celebrate the Muslim New Year, the Bianou festival is held in the city of Agadez to commemorate the birth of the prophet Mohammed and the mysterious construction of the Great Mosque of Agadez. It is celebrated for three days and starts with *ettebel* ("ET-bel"), a drumming and a call from the minaret. As the crowds gather, the *ettebel* players appear, followed by Tuareg dancers who perform spinning dances in their long, blue robes.

The festival is held in the sultan's palace. Tuaregs from neighboring cities come to take part in the grand camel race, which includes more than 200 camels with traditionally dressed Tuaregs. To start the camel race, women musicians play *tindé*. The race begins outside the city, and the finish line is the courtyard at the sultan's palace. In the evening, crowds gather to listen to a *takamba* ("TAH-kahm-ba") performance, music played by a traditional guitar player. Women start to gather in a circle, and the men start dancing. The women then join in the dance.

109

Seasonal rain in Teguidda-n-Tessoum. Some time after this period, between July and September, the Salt Cure Festival will start.

SALT CURE FESTIVAL

Every winter, the Bororo Fulani and the Tuareg nomads gather after completing a year-long seasonal migration and hold the Salt Cure Festival in In-Gall and Teguidda-n-Tessoum, where green pastures are abundant. In-Gall is located in an oasis with palm groves and date plantations. The name "salt cure" comes from salt contained in the new grass. The salt diet is essential to animals. The nomads believe that the salt cure fattens the animals.

During the festival, the Tuaregs, dressed in traditional clothes, hold camel races, and artisans exhibit their exquisite leather and wooden artifacts, and their jewelry. To offer support, the government regularly takes part in the celebration by distributing sugar, millet, and tea to the nomads. To kick off the celebrations, Tuareg women play *tindé* and sing. While they perform, the men proudly ride their camels around the racing grounds.

The Bororo group of the Fulani also hold their annual beauty contest at this time. Called the *Gerewol*, the cult of beauty reaches its apex during this celebration, in which only men are allowed to participate. After spending many long hours doning traditional make-up and decorating themselves with their most beautiful clothes and jewelry, the Bororo men line up to perform a dance.

The participants, who have decorated their faces with pale yellow powder and painted the edges of their eyes with black kohl, dance forward, graciously shifting and lifting their weight from one foot to the other while clapping their hands and singing. As they dance, they will smile at a group of young unmarried women who are the judges. It is customary for the dancers to keep their eyes wide open to emphasize their facial beauty. After the dance, the judges mix with the young men and choose the most beautiful. However, if the men are displeased with the judges' decision, fights can break out. The Nigerien government has attempted to stop this celebration because it often ends in violence.

Bororo men, with their painted faces and decorative dress, get ready to dance during *Gerewol*.

YENENDI

Yenendi is a rain-calling traditional ceremony where the worshippers request that the earth be showered with the rains before the fields are planted. It is usually performed when there is a drought. The ceremony is called for by the village spokesman who invites the villagers to gather around a sacred place outside the village, usually held under a big gao tree. The barefooted *Bori* cult followers wear masks and are dressed in black clothes and black hats. When the ceremony starts, spirits are summoned to bring rain to relieve the thirsty land. A sacrifice of small animals usually takes place, along with a spirit possession. This is followed by a procession around the village. All the villagers join in the procession, dancing and singing while waiting for the rain to come.

WRESTLING CHAMPIONSHIP

With the help of the Ministry of Sports and Culture, the championship games for traditional wrestling have become the most popular sport among Nigeriens. Traditional Nigerien wrestling is the forte of the sedentary Hausa, and attract many fans every time the games are held. Established in 1975, the championship games draw large crowds to the wrestling grounds. Television and radio viewership also reaches a peak during the games.

Nigerien wrestling is somewhat different from the common forms of wrestling. It is more a mix of Japanese sumo wrestling and Greco-Roman wrestling. At an early age, children in the rural areas start practicing, but the strongest wrestlers come from urban areas. The winner may not always be the heaviest or strongest. Besides physical training, preparation for the wrestling championship includes psychological exercises, animist rituals, and prayers. The sport is also practiced in several West African countries.

The preliminary selection of contestants is held in the morning in the administrative centers of the territorial départements. Each département holds its own games and selects a 10-member team that will represent it on the national level. The national championship takes a week to complete. During the championship games, besides the matches, wrestlers parade in the arena, showing their muscles, while musicians entertain the spectators, and the camel riders perform their camel dance.

To win the championship, the wrestler must win seven rounds. One round is won when his opponent falls on the sand. The winner is awarded a sword, a horse with a harness, a traditional outfit, and a check that he receives from the hands of the Nigerien Minister of Youth and Sports.

MAJOR SECULAR HOLIDAYS

Most Nigeriens do not work on New Year's Day, which falls on January 1. However, as most of them are Muslims and celebrate only the Muslim New Year, the Christian New Year is just a public holiday for them, not an important occasion. Easter Monday, Labor Day (May 1), and the Proclamation of the Republic (December 1) are national holidays. Other important celebrations are on April 15, which commemorates the coup that ousted Diori; August 3, the anniversary of independence; and December 18, Republic Day, which is the republic's birthday.

FOOD

THE TRADITIONAL CUISINE OF NIGER is varied. By using only staples such as millet and sorghum, Nigerien women are able to create several delicious dishes for every meal. The flavors and tastes of each dish can be very different for the various ethnic groups.

STAPLES

Millet is Niger's main staple. The traditional midday meal is *fura* ("FOO-rah"), a millet porridge prepared with water or milk, spices, and cooked flour. The pastoral Fulani rely on dairy products, such as yogurt, milk, and butter, but also eat millet, sorghum, and corn porridge. Besides millet, the Hausa diet also consists of sorghum and corn. The Tuareg nomads eat mainly cereals. Dairy products, such as milk and cheese, and fruits, like dates and melons, provide additional nutrition.

Left: **Food vendors selling staples.**

Opposite: **A Tuareg nomad prepares *taguila* ("tah-GOO-ee-lah), a type of flatbread.**

115

A butcher working on an animal skin that he has removed from an animal, while two other butchers take a break.

MEAT AND VEGETABLES

Nigeriens like to eat meat. When available, it is frequently consumed, particularly by the Tuareg. Nigeriens prepare meat dishes mainly during special occasions and holidays. In markets, grilled mutton brochettes are popular snacks as they provide energy. Fresh or dried vegetables, such as okra, onions, peppers, spinach, tomatoes, squash, pumpkins, eggplant, sorrel, and baobab leaves, are added to sauces or porridge. Fish is a favorite among the people who live near the Niger River and Lake Chad. Nigeriens enjoy snacks prepared with meat and grilled tripe, and cakes made with fried beans or peanuts. In season, mangoes, dates, and melons are usually consumed in large quantities.

The different ethnic groups have different food and table customs. The Fulani consume meat but do not slaughter their cows. The Songhai men and women eat separately. To increase children's food consumption, the custom is to eat from the same gourds. During the cricket season, women snack on fried crickets, referred to as "desert shrimps."

TRADITIONAL MEALS

Nigeriens' traditional meals consist largely of porridge, pancakes, or
pastes from millet flour. Pancakes are eaten at breakfast, porridge at noon,
and pastes topped with other ingredients and sauces are consumed in
the evening.

A normal midday meal in a rural or poor urban family consists of
boiled millet or sorghum, and buttermilk. Sometimes spices or sugar are
added. In the evening, *tô* ("TOH"), a popular West African dish made with
white millet or sorghum balls, is eaten with different kinds of sauces. The
sauces are made from green leaves, onions, tomatoes, dried legumes,
spices, and meat, if any. If there is chicken, dried beans and sorghum
usually complement the dish. In the rice-planting region along the Niger
River, rice is eaten with local spices and spinach-like herbs and groundnuts.
Dishes with smoked or dried fish are cooked with local ingredients. Most
rural families have two meals a day. For the poorer ones, one meal per day
is common.

In urban areas, wealthy families lead a more Westernized lifestyle. They also have the opportunity to try Western food. For them, a traditional meal means plenty of rice prepared with a tasty vegetable sauce and eaten with meat or fish. In contrast to the rural people, urban families can afford to have three meals a day.

The eating habits of the nomads in Niger are similar to those of the farmers. The main difference is that, compared to their fellow countrymen, they consume more milk and dairy products, such as butter. The dairy products are produced from cow's milk, which is also used to trade for cereals. The nomads also eat a substantial amount of meat, because from time to time, they slaughter some animals from their herds.

Opposite: **Some of the various spices that Nigeriens eat.**

Below: **An outdoor restaurant in Niamey.**

NIGERIEN FOOD TRADITIONS

Families supplement their regular meals by eating raw roots, tubers, manioc, and sweet potatoes. Fruits and vegetables are expensive, and meat, eggs, and fish are only prepared during family celebrations and holidays.

Depending on the ethnic groups and their socioeconomic conditions, religions forbid the consumption of some foods, such as pork and alcohol. The meat also has to be fresh, and the animal must be slaughtered in accordance with Islamic principles. Tradition forbids pregnant women and children from eating certain foods too, such as eggs.

SIPPING TEA

In many Muslim countries in Africa, a traditional custom is to drink hot and foamy tea. To the Tuareg, tea drinking is a solemn affair. It is a ceremonial display where each step of the preparation is carried out with care. In addition to its dehydrating and stimulant properties, tea offers drinkers an opportunity to hold long conversations, especially near a campfire while enjoying the starry desert night. To make tea, two pots are used. The steaming tea is poured from one pot to the other, so that a foam appears. The foam protects the drinker's lips.

DRINKS

Among the Tuareg, *aragaiga* ("ah-RAH-gay-gah") tea, which is Chinese green tea, is the preferred drink after a meal. Mint is usually added to the tea, and three cups are always drunk. The Tuareg say that the first cup of tea is strong, the second cup is soft, which means it is slightly weaker than the first, and the third cup is light and is usually offered to the children. During special ceremonies and on journeys, the Tuareg drink *egherdjira* ("ER-er-jee-rah"), a drink prepared with pounded millet, dates, milk, and goat cheese. It is very rich and is drunk with a ladle.

In the cities, people sip strong, hot coffee for breakfast. Sometimes the coffee is mixed with milk. The Nigerien Dairy Company produces buttermilk and light milk. Soft drinks, found at every food outlet, are popular. They include Coca-Cola, Sprite, Fanta, and local soft drinks produced by a Nigerien soft drink company called Bra-Niger. The company also produces the local alcoholic beer, although Islam forbids its followers from drinking alcohol.

In the villages, a local alcoholic drink, *bourkoutou* ("BOOR-koo-too"), made by fermenting millet, is very strong and is favored by the Hausa. In the large cities, such as Niamey, French-owned stores carry food products specially imported from Europe. As these products, such as yogurt and ice cream, are very expensive, few Nigeriens can afford to enjoy them.

A TYPICAL NIGERIEN SAUCE

cooking oil
1 onion, chopped
1 pound of mutton or goat meat, cut into small pieces
3 tomatoes, sliced
$\frac{1}{4}$ medium cabbage, shredded
salt and pepper
hot pepper
cilantro
cumin seeds
coriander
garlic, chopped
curry powder
thyme
oregano
lime juice or lemon juice
water

Heat the oil. Fry the chopped onion and the meat in a little oil, then add the sliced tomatoes. Cover and simmer the mixture for two to three minutes. Add the cabbage, then cover and cook on low fire for five minutes. Sprinkle some salt and pepper to taste. Add the spices and herbs. Pour in some water if you want a lighter sauce. Serve over rice, thick cornmeal, pounded yam, or flatbread.

Less well-off Nigeriens cannot afford to provide nutritious meals for their children. In rural areas, breast milk is the children's only food supply. Therefore mothers usually breast-feed their children until they reach 2 or 3 years of age.

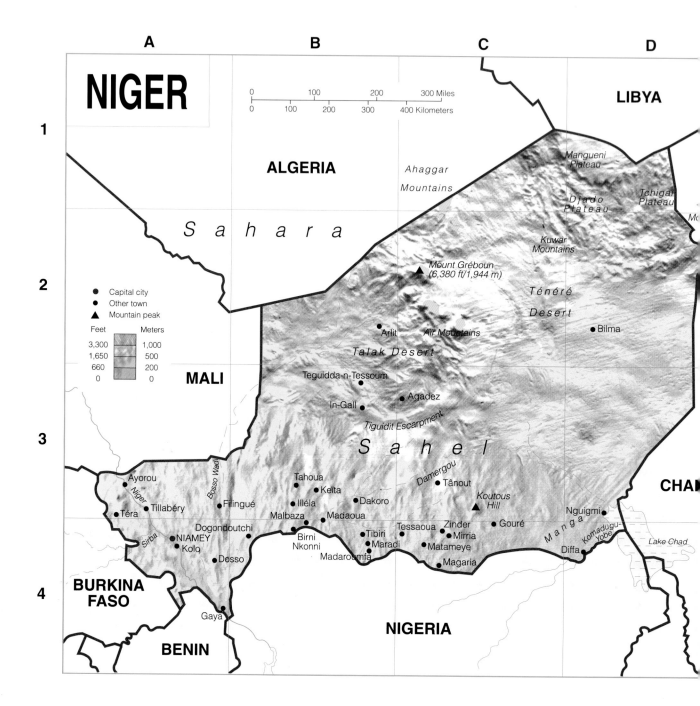

NIGER

A	B	C	D

0 100 200 300 Miles
0 100 200 300 400 Kilometers

LIBYA

ALGERIA

S a h a r a

Ahaggar Mountains

Mangueni Plateau

Djado Plateau

Tchigaï Plateau

Kuwar Mountains

▲ Mount Gréboun
(6,380 ft/1,944 m)

Ténéré Desert

● Capital city
● Other town
▲ Mountain peak

Feet	Meters
3,300	1,000
1,650	500
660	200
0	0

MALI

● Arlit   *Air Mountains*   ● Bilma

Talak Desert

Teguidda-n-Tessoum ●

In-Gall ●   ● Agadez

Tiguidit Escarpment

S a h e l

Damergou

● Tânout

Koutous Hill ▲

CHA

Ayorou ●
● Tillabéry
Niger
Filingué ●

Tahoua ●
● Keïta
● Illéla   ● Dakoro
Malbaza ● Madaoua

Bosso Wadi

Nguigmi ●

Manga

● Téra

Dogondoutchi ●
● NIAMEY
● Kolo
Sirba

Birni Nkonni ●

● Tibiri
● Maradi

Tessaoua ● Zinder ●
● Mirria   ● Gouré
● Matameye

Komadugu-Yobe

Lake Chad

● Dosso

Madaroumfa ●

● Magaria

Diffa ●

BURKINA FASO

Gaya ●

BENIN

NIGERIA

122

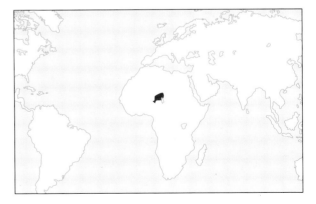

QUICK NOTES

OFFICIAL NAME
Republic of Niger

TOTAL AREA
489,062 square miles (1,267,000 square km)

POPULATION
9,962,242 people (July 1999 estimate)

POPULATION GROWTH RATE
2.95% (July 1999 estimate)

CAPITAL
Niamey

**ADMINISTRATIVE DIVISIONS
(*DÉPARTMENTS*)**
Agadez, Diffa, Dosso, Maradi, Niamey, Tahoua,
Tillabéry, Zinder

NATURAL HAZARDS
Recurring droughts

CLIMATE
Desert; mostly hot, dry, dusty; tropical in
extreme south

HIGHEST POINT
Mount Gréboun (6,380 feet/1,944 m)

CURRENCY
Communaute Financière Africaine franc (CFAF)
US$1= 608.36 CFAF (1998)

MAJOR IMPORTS
Consumer goods, primary materials, machin-
ery, vehicles and parts, petroleum, and cereals

MAJOR EXPORTS
Uranium ore, livestock products, cowpeas,
onions

ETHNIC GROUPS
Hausa (56%), Songhai-Djerma (22%), Fulani
(8.5%), Tuareg (8%), Kanouri (4.3%), Arab,
Toubou, and Gourmantche (1.2%), French
expatriates (about 1,200)

MAJOR LANGUAGES
French (official), Hausa, Djerma

LITERACY RATE
13.6%

RELIGIONS
Muslims (80%), indigenous beliefs, and
Christians.

INDEPENDENCE DAY
August 3, 1960

NATIONAL HOLIDAY
Republic Day (December 18)

HEAD OF STATE
President Daouda Malam Wanké

GLOSSARY

Ajami ("ah-JAH-mee")
Modified Arabic script formerly used by the Hausa. It means "non-Arab" or "foreigner."

Amazigh ("ah-mah-ZEER")
Refers to the Berbers. The word means "noble man."

azalay ("ah-ZAH-lay")
Long annual camel salt caravans that traverse the Ténéré Desert.

Bori ("BOH-ree")
Ancient ritual possession cult practiced by a group of Hausa.

dara ("da-RAH")
A checker-like game played with pits of the dum-dum tree fruit and short millet twigs.

Gerewol ("GER-e-wol")
A week-long festival with dances and a male beauty contest held by the Bororo Fulani.

griot ("GREE-yaw")
Local bard, poet, narrator, and musician.

hajj ("HAHJ")
The pilgrimage to Mecca.

hidjab ("hee-JAB")
A piece of cloth worn by a Muslim woman. It covers the entire body except the eyes.

imam ("EE-mahm")
A Muslim religious figure who preaches at a mosque.

magajiya ("mah-GAH-jee-yah")
Bori queen, who leads the women to be initiated in the *Bori* ritual.

sharro ("SHAR-raw")
A sport-like activity that tests the endurance and bravery of Fulani teenagers.

tagelmust ("tag-ERL-moost")
A piece of long, indigo cotton cloth worn by the Tuareg men to veil themselves.

teneghelt ("te-NER-gelt")
A term used by the Tuaregs. It refers to the silver cross of Agadez.

Tifinagh ("tee-FEE-nahr")
An ancient script of the Berber language still used by the Tuaregs.

tindé ("TUHN-day")
Musical rhythm created by a tambourine-like instrument made with a mortar and goat skin stretched across the opening and attached with strings to two pieces of wood.

yenendi ("yay-NAN-dee")
A traditional ritual to summon rain when the rains fail to come at the end of the dry season.

BIBLIOGRAPHY

Ayaji, J.F.A. & Crowder, Michael. *History of West Africa* (Vol. 1, 3rd edition). Longman Group, 1985.

Delgado, Samuel. *Historical Dictionary of Niger*. New Jersey: Scarecrow Press, Inc., 1996.

Hale, Thomas A. *Griots and Griottes: Masters of Words and Music*. Indiana University Press, 1999.

Keenan, Jeremy. *The Tuareg*. New York: St. Martin's Press, 1977.

Malio, Nouhou & Maiga, Mounkaila & Thomas A. Hale (editor). *The Epic of Askia Mohammed (African Epic Series)*. Indiana University Press, 1996.

Manning, Patrick. *Francophone Sub-Saharan Africa: 1180–1995*. Cambridge University Press, 1998.

Offelen, Van & Beckwith, Marion & Carol. *Nomads of Niger*. New York: Abradale Press, 1993.

Riesman, Paul. *Freedom in Fulani Social Life*. Chicago: University of Chicago Press, 1977.

INDEX

INDEX

INDEX